WHY SMALL groups?

TOGETHER TOWARD MATURITY

EDITED BY C.J. MAHANEY

Executive Editor: Greg Somerville

Associate Editor: Kevin Meath

SOVEREIGN GRACE® MINISTRIES
The Pursuit *of* Godliness Series

Sovereign Grace Media is a division of Sovereign Grace Ministries,
which serves a growing network of local churches in the United States
and abroad. For information about the ministry or for permission to
reproduce portions of this book, please contact us.

Sovereign Grace Ministries
7505 Muncaster Mill Road
Gaithersburg, MD 20877

800.736.2202
fax: 301.948.7833
info@sovgracemin.org
www.SovereignGraceMinistries.org

WHY SMALL GROUPS?

General Editor: C.J. Mahaney
Cover design: Gallison Design (www.gallisondesign.com)
Book layout: Martin Stanley

ISBN 13 978-1-881039-06-8
ISBN 10 1-881039-06-4

Printed in the United States of America

0211c

CONTENTS

HOW TO USE THIS BOOK

Why Small Groups?, like each book in the Pursuit of Godliness series, is designed for group and individual use. The series is the logical outgrowth of four deeply held convictions:

■ The Bible is our infallible standard for faith, doctrine, and practice. Those who resist its authority will be blown off course by their own feelings and cultural trends.

■ Knowledge without application is lifeless. In order to be transformed, we must apply and practice the truth of God's Word in daily life.

■ Application of these principles is impossible apart from the Holy Spirit. While we must participate in change, he is the source of our power.

■ The church is God's intended context for change. God never intended for us to live isolated from or independent of other Christians. Through committed participation in the local church, we find instruction, encouragement, correction, and opportunities to press on toward maturity in Christ.

As you work through these pages, we trust each of these foundational convictions will be reinforced in your heart.

With the possible exception of the "Group Discussion" questions, the format of this book is equally suited for individuals and small groups. A variety of different elements have been included to make each chapter as interesting and helpful as possible. For those of you who can't get enough of a particular topic, we've listed at the end of each chapter one or more additional books that will help you grow in the Lord.

While you are encouraged to experiment in your use of this book, group discussion will be better served when members work through the material in advance. And remember that you're not going through this book alone. The Holy Spirit is your tutor. With his help, this book has the potential to change your life.

FOREWORD

Some might be wondering, "Why another book on small groups?" Actually, we would prefer that a book like this weren't necessary, but it clearly is. Though there seems to be an endless supply of books written about and for small groups, we have found little that 1) contains sound doctrine, 2) is written by pastors, and 3) places a biblical emphasis on the local church. So you hold in your hands our small contribution. We hope it is helpful.

Participating in this project was a real joy because of its purpose and content. No less significant was the honor of working with men I deeply respect. Each of the men who contributed to this book is passionate about God, the local church, and small groups. I believe that will be evident as you read each chapter. What may not be evident is the sacrifices they have made over the years to train and care for God's people.

You won't find theories in this book; you'll find biblical principles that have been put into practice by the authors since the early 1980s. For this I would like to thank each of the authors. Apart from their effective service and leadership, this book would not be possible. Special thanks to Greg Somerville, not only for his fine chapter but for his excellent editing skills as well.

This book is dedicated to all the small-group leaders in the churches we have had the privilege to serve. You have been exemplary in your passion for God, your commitment to the local church, your support of your pastors, and your care for God's people. We thank God for each of you! And we can't thank you enough for the difference you make. It is a distinct privilege to serve our Lord and his purpose with you.

Soli Deo Gloria!

— **C.J. Mahaney**

ABOUT THE AUTHORS

C.J. MAHANEY leads Sovereign Grace Ministries in its mission to establish and support local churches with the gospel, for the glory of God. He pastored Covenant Life Church (Gaithersburg, MD) for 27 years before handing that role to Joshua Harris in order to devote his full attention to Sovereign Grace. C.J.'s books include *Humility: True Greatness*; *Living the Cross-Centered Life*; and *Sex, Romance, and the Glory of God: What Every Christian Husband Needs to Know*. He also edited or coauthored four books in the Pursuit of Godliness book series.

JOHN LOFTNESS credits his wife, Nancy, with first showing him how to ask the questions—and listen to the answers—that lead to true, biblical fellowship. John, a former schoolteacher, principal, and editor of *Sovereign Grace* magazine, has served Covenant Life Church as a pastor full-time since 1989. He and Nancy have four children and live in Gaithersburg, Maryland.

GREG SOMERVILLE served as executive editor of *Sovereign Grace* magazine and was the original executive editor for this book series. He now serves on the pastoral team and oversees day school and homeschool programs at Covenant Life Church (Gaithersburg, MD), where he and his wife, Suzy, (along with their six children) are members. Greg is indebted to the men and women of his small group, whose support and enthusiastic participation have made the years rich with memories.

MARK MULLERY served as a small-group leader, and later as senior pastor, of Abundant Life Community Church in Pasadena, California. He now serves as senior pastor of Sovereign Grace Church in Fairfax, Virginia. Mark enjoys nothing more than personally discovering and teaching others about God's amazing grace. He and his wife, Lesley, have four children.

MICKEY CONNOLLY serves as senior pastor of CrossWay Community Church in Charlotte, North Carolina, having first served for six years as senior pastor of Solid Rock Church in Riverdale, Maryland. He and his wife, Jane, have three children. Over the years Mickey has learned, slowly but surely, to appreciate the value of giving and receiving biblical correction. He fully expects that learning curve to continue indefinitely.

JOHN BUTLER had served for several years as a small-group leader and pastor when God called him to help pastor a new church in Chesapeake, Virginia, now known as Sovereign Grace Church. He now serves as senior pastor of Sovereign Grace Church in Kennesaw, Georgia. John and his wife, Beverly, have two children.

DAVE HARVEY experienced one test of his commitment to church life years ago when he lingered in a low-paying job in order to stay involved in a vibrant local church. Eventually, God directed him to move to Philadelphia to join a new church-planting venture. Soon he was leading a small group. Now Dave is senior pastor of Covenant Fellowship Church in Glen Mills, Pennsylvania, and a member of the Sovereign Grace leadership team. Dave and his wife, Kimm, live in West Chester, Pennsylvania, with their four children.

CHAPTER ONE

WHY SMALL GROUPS?

C.J. MAHANEY

"You see, but you do not observe," said Sherlock Holmes to his loyal friend, Dr. Watson. "The distinction is clear. For example, you have frequently seen the steps which lead up from the hall to this room."

"Frequently."

"How often?"

"Well, some hundreds of times."

"Then how many are there?"

"How many? I don't know."

"Quite so! You have not observed. And yet you have seen. This is just my point. Now, I know that there are seventeen steps, because I have both seen and observed."[1]

If you have read any of Sir Arthur Conan Doyle's classic detective stories, you know that Sherlock Holmes often rebukes Dr. Watson for his oversight. But Watson was no fool. Like me, and probably you, he simply lacked Holmes' unusually strong gifts of observation and deduction. He could see the very same situations as Holmes without gaining the same depth of understanding. As Holmes stated, Watson saw…but he did not observe.

By the way, if I had been in Watson's place, I might have answered the famous detective a bit differently. I would at least have been tempted to say, "How many steps? Who cares! Just solve the case, pal."

But Sherlock Holmes was acutely aware of the need to "observe"—to see beyond the obvious. As we examine the subject of small groups, it's crucial that we, too, see beyond the obvious. We need to seek an understanding more sophisticated than, "This is a staircase," or "This is a group of people meeting in a home." We must go deeper, to grasp the real purpose of small groups. We need to know why we meet, and what it means to make a meaningful contribution. We need to know why our small group exists.

Because if we don't know God's purpose for small groups, we're never going to achieve it.

Small Groups Are Elementary, My Dear Watson

Meditate on Matthew 7:24-27. What does Jesus promise to those who build on the foundation of his Word?

Since the mid-1970s, the church in America has been fascinated with small groups. The majority of churches have at least experimented with small groups, and many maintain active small-group ministries of various kinds.

However, from my limited perspective, a number of these churches never hammered out a clear purpose and set of biblical goals when beginning their small groups. Some did, and it is these churches that no doubt have had the greatest success with their small groups. But others started groups simply because they were popular—the latest church trend. Obviously, that isn't a sufficient motive. Current trends rarely provide a church with strong foundations. A small-group ministry won't ultimately be effective unless it exists to achieve biblical purposes.

For lack of a biblical purpose and mandate, many small groups have floundered. Other groups have been seriously handicapped by the lack of good resources available. It is no exaggeration to say that most popular books and guides dealing with the topic of small groups are shockingly deficient in sound doctrine. I don't say this lightly. I have reviewed them for years, and have found a greater emphasis on modern psychology and sociology than on biblical theology.

Most of these materials are well-produced. They feature numerous thought-provoking questions and illustrations. Undoubtedly the publishers want to help Christians grow. But without solid biblical content, these materials can actually hinder God's intentions for us as individuals and groups.

Despite these concerns, I see small groups as a priority for every Christian and every church. Why? Because the Scripture constantly underscores the centrality of relationships. J.I. Packer agrees:

> We should not think of our fellowship with other Christians as a spiritual luxury, an optional addition to the exercises of private devotions. Fellowship is one of the great words of the New Testament: it denotes something that is vital to a Christian's spiritual health, and central to the Church's true life…The church will flourish and Christians will be strong only when there is fellowship.[2]

For Further Study:
Read 1 John 1:7.
How ought Christians to relate to one another in order to experience fellowship?

Genuine fellowship isn't practical in a crowd of 200 or 2,000. That's why I feel so strongly that churches must create small groups where Christians can develop strong, personal relationships, where they can "know and be known." A church following a biblical model will not just "have" small groups. It will not merely "offer" small groups. Rather, it will *be built with* small groups.

As I stated before, though, small groups will only serve the church if they are founded on sound doctrine and sustained by a clear biblical purpose. That brings us to the title of this chapter and this book: *Why Small Groups?*

To answer the question posed by that title, let me present what I consider to be four clear goals from Scripture: progressive sanctification, mutual care, fellowship, and the ministry of the Holy Spirit.

What Sanctification Is—and Is Not

Theologian Wayne Grudem provides a fine, concise definition of this critical doctrine: "Sanctification is a progressive work of God and man that makes us more and more free from sin and like Christ in our actual lives."[3] That's the goal of the Christian life, isn't it? Increasing freedom from sin and increasing resemblance to Jesus. Small groups provide an ideal context for this to occur.

Not every small group is intent on this purpose, however. Some put a higher priority on socializing than on sanctification. Others excel in open sharing and sympathetic listening, yet they never confront sin or challenge members to change.

This is unacceptable. A group with a less-than-biblical purpose can do more harm than good. Groups that meet without the biblical purpose of pursuing character development have the tendency to reinforce, rather than confront, the sin and selfishness already present in us. None of us needs such reinforcement. Instead, we need to be provoked and challenged by others so we can grow in spiritual maturity, for the glory of God.

Let me make one critical insertion here before going any further. I've spoken with many Christians who don't understand the difference

1 If someone in your group pointed out what she thought was a sin in your life (without first getting written permission), how would you respond?

❏ Become offended but internalize it

❏ Become offended and express it

❏ Dissolve into tears

❏ Point out the obvious sins in her life

❏ Thank her for her care and concern

between the doctrine of sanctification and the doctrine of justification. Because this confusion can lead to serious spiritual consequences, let me take a minute to distinguish these critical truths. Please follow closely—the rest of this book (and the rest of your Christian life!) depends on a clear understanding of these two doctrines.

I have given Dr. Grudem's definition of sanctification above. He defines the doctrine of justification this way:

> Justification is an instantaneous legal act of God in which he 1) thinks of our sins as forgiven and Christ's righteousness as belonging to us, and 2) declares us to be righteous in his sight.[4]

Justification refers to a Christian's *position* before God. The moment you were born again, God justified you. On the basis of Christ's finished work, God thought of your sins as forgiven and declared that you were righteous.

Sanctification, on the other hand, refers to our *practice* before God. It is the ongoing process of battling sin and becoming more like Jesus. Though sanctification is the evidence and goal of our justification, we must never see it as the basis of our justification. Here's where so many Christians get confused. They try to earn what has already been given to them as a free gift. As Martin Luther stated, "The only contribution we make to our justification is our sin which God so graciously forgives."

There are other vital distinctions. Justification is about being declared righteous; sanctification is about becoming more righteous. Justification is immediate; sanctification is gradual. Justification is complete the moment God declares us righteous. It does not take place by degrees. Sanctification, however, is a process that lasts as long as we live. Finally, while every Christian enjoys the same degree of justification, we vary in terms of sanctification. You will never be more justified than you are at this moment, because justification is an act of God. But by God's grace, you will become ever more sanctified as you cooperate with God's Spirit in the process of change.

Though it's important to distinguish between justification and sanctification, these two doctrines are

Meditate on Romans 5:1-2. In three words, summarize the benefit of justification that you find described in this passage.

> 66 The glory of the gospel is that God has declared Christians to be rightly related to him in spite of their sin. But our greatest temptation and mistake is to try to smuggle character into his work of grace. How easily we fall into the trap of assuming that we only remain justified so long as there are grounds in our character for that justification. But Paul's teaching is that nothing we do ever contributes to our justification.[5] 99
>
> — **Sinclair Ferguson**

inseparable. God does not justify someone without sanctifying him as well. Sanctification is not optional. If one has truly been justified, that will be evident by a progressive work of sanctification in his life. Small groups contribute to this magnificent and gradual work of grace in our lives.

Don't Try This Alone

Meditate on Hebrews 10:24-25. How have you benefitted from having others "spur you on" in the faith?

Although one's personal responsibility for sanctification is paramount, sanctification cannot be accomplished in isolation from the local church. Scripture clearly teaches that sanctification is intended to take place in the local church—and small groups contribute invaluably to this process. Consider these insights by theologian Bruce Milne:

> The Christian life is inescapably corporate. Teaching on Christian holiness has frequently concentrated almost exclusively on the "holy man" or the "holy woman," to the neglect of the biblical concern for "the holy people" or the "holy church." The ideal of the "omnicompetent Christian individual," able to meet every spiritual challenge and live a life of unbroken victory over sin and the devil, has undoubtedly produced remarkable examples of Christian character; but, as every Christian counsellor knows, this emphasis has driven many to a lonely struggle ending in despair and disillusionment, or, worse, in the hypocrisy of a double-standard life.
>
> This whole approach needs re-examination. The bulk of New Testament teaching on the Christian life, including the major sections on holiness, occur in letters addressed to corporate groups, to churches. All the major exhortations to holy living are plural— "we," "you" (Ro 6:1-23; Gal 5:13-6:10; Eph 4:17-6:18)...Similarly all the New Testament promises of victory are corporate (1Co 15:57; 1Jn 5:4; Rev 15:2). In other words the apostles envisaged the Christian life and Christian sanctification in the context of a loving, caring fellowship.[6]

For Further Study: According to Ephesians 4:15, what two ingredients must be present in our communication with other Christians?

By the grace of God, I've experienced what Milne is describing. Many of the most significant changes in my Christian life have taken place in the fellowship of the local church—specifically, in small groups. On many occasions, members of my small group have lovingly confronted my sin and held me accountable as I pursued change. Of course, the Holy Spirit is directly responsible for convicting me of these things, but I can only guess where I would be without such faithful friends. God has used them time after time to address sins in my life that I would never have perceived were I not an active member of a local church.

There is a common yet false supposition among Christians that practicing the spiritual disciplines (prayer, memorizing and meditating on Scripture, fasting, confession of sin, etc.) is sufficient to maintain spiritual growth. But as vital as these practices are, they are not sufficient. Small groups provide the encouragement, correction, and accountability that are necessary to keep us from drifting. We need others to help us in our pursuit of sanctification.

> **❝** It is both foolish and wicked to suppose that we will make much progress in sanctification if we isolate ourselves from the visible church. Indeed, it is commonplace to hear people declare that they don't need to unite with a church to be a Christian. They claim that their devotion is personal and private, not institutional or corporate. This is not the testimony of the great saints of history; it is the confession of fools.[7] **❞**
>
> **— R.C. Sproul**

If you have a passion for personal change—and every Christian should—then you will be glad when others challenge you to grow. This should not be seen as abnormal, or as the domain of those with an unusual level of maturity. It should be viewed as the normal process that follows new birth, expressed in a desire to conform to the image of Jesus Christ. We should be seriously and unapologetically committed to change.

Who Is Your Nathan?

Cain, when questioned by God about the murder of Abel, tried to deny he was his brother's keeper (Ge 4:9). But he was. We all are. We have a responsibility to help our brothers and sisters keep the will of God. The common term for this is accountability. It is a specific way in which relationships help us pursue sanctification.

An accountability relationship is "one in which a Christian gives permission to another believer to look into his life for purposes of questioning, challenging, admonishing, advising, encouraging, and otherwise providing input in ways that will help the individual live according to the Christian principles that they both hold. The relationship involves confession and prayer. The relationship may be one-way—as when a person becomes accountable

THESE GUYS MEANT *BUSINESS!*

Early in the 18th century, Samuel Wesley (brother of John Wesley) formed a religious society with regular small-group meetings. Called "Band Societies," these single-sex groups were designed to facilitate mutual accountability. All who wished to join were required to answer the following questions as evidence of justification and an accompanying desire to grow in God:

Have you peace with God through our Lord Jesus Christ?

Do you desire to be told of your faults?

Do you desire that every one of us should tell you, from time to time, whatsoever is in his heart concerning you?

Consider! Do you desire that we should tell you whatsoever we think, whatsoever we fear, whatsoever we hear, concerning you?

Do you desire that, in doing this, we should come as close as possible, that we should cut to the quick, and search your heart to the bottom?

Is it your desire and design to be on this, and all other occasions, entirely open, so as to speak everything that is in your heart without exception, without disguise, and without reserve?

After joining, group members could be asked the preceding questions "as often as occasion offers," while the following questions were asked at every meeting:

What known sin have you committed since our last meeting?

What temptations have you met with?

How were you delivered?

What have you thought, said, or done, of which you doubt whether it be sin or not?[8]

to an elder in the church—or it may be mutual—the two parties are accountable to one another. Or the accountability may involve a small group."[9]

The lives of King David and his son Solomon illustrate the importance of being accountable. When David committed adultery with Bathsheba and had her husband killed, David was confronted—held accountable—by the prophet Nathan (see 2 Samuel 11-12). As a result, he repented of his sin and received God's forgiveness. What would David have become without Nathan in his life?

Solomon, on the other hand, apparently had no one like Nathan to hold him accountable as he began to disobey God's commands. Eventually he was severely disciplined by God for his sin. What might Solomon have become with someone like Nathan in his life? A more relevant question is, what will you become without a Nathan in your life?

Take it from Solomon: "Two are better than one, because they have a good return for their work: If one falls down, his friend can help him up. But pity the man who falls and has no one to help him up" (Ecc 4:9-10). The man speaks from experience. If Solomon—the wisest man who had ever lived—needed accountability, then each of us does as well.

Is there someone who can (and does) question your

For Further Study:
The tragic account of Solomon's spiritual decline is found in 1 Kings 11:1-13.

motives and ask for an explanation of your actions when appropriate? This is what we want to work toward in our small groups. Like Wesley's Band Societies (see "These Guys Meant *Business!*" on page 7), we want our small-group meetings to fulfill Proverbs 27:17: "As iron sharpens iron so one man sharpens another." Even as we rest fully secure in our justification before God because of the substitutionary sacrifice of the Son, let us be passionate in our pursuit of sanctification.

Mirror, Mirror, On the Wall

Relationships are one vital means of sanctification; God's Word is another. Nothing changes us more effectively than the grace-motivated application of Scripture. I'm aware of this every time I preach. What a sobering responsibility! And yet I'm also aware that my words—no matter how passionately I deliver them or how persuasive they may seem—will often fail to bear fruit. That's because merely hearing God's Word is insufficient. It bears fruit only when we apply it. And as we'll see in a minute, small groups are an ideal context for applying God's Word.

The Book of James uses a humorous illustration to show the importance of application:

> Do not merely listen to the word, and so deceive yourselves. Do what it says. Anyone who listens to the word but does not do what it says is like a man who looks at his face in a mirror and, after looking at himself, goes away and immediately forgets what he looks like. (Jas 1:22-24)

I don't know anybody who wakes up in the morning, looks in the mirror, and then leaves the house without making some strategic changes. In fact, most of us spend considerable time in front of the mirror each morning—assessing the damages from the night before and making the necessary repairs. According to an article I once saw in *Newsweek*, a typical man's lifetime will include a total of seven years in the bathroom.[10] Much of that time will be spent looking in the mirror as we make increasingly futile attempts at damage control.

Meditate on Hebrews 4:12. Once you apply God's Word to your life, you'll find that it has a unique power to change you!

Wouldn't you be just a little concerned if you knew someone who got up each day, looked in the mirror, and walked away without making any adjustments? How long would that person be presentable to others? How long would you wait before you offered him a comb? It's an

2 Can you identify one verse or passage from the Bible that has provoked you to change? Briefly summarize what it says in the space below.

absurd scenario…or is it? According to James, this is exactly what happens every time we encounter Scripture (the mirror) and then walk away without making any changes.

The person who routinely looks in the mirror without making alterations does not understand the purpose of the mirror. Likewise, the person who reads or listens to God's Word without applying what he has heard obviously doesn't understand the purpose of Scripture.

Simply reading your Bible and listening to good preaching won't make you more like Jesus. Though each of these disciplines is essential for the Christian life and each is a vital means of grace, neither is sufficient in itself. In fact, biblical knowledge is potentially deceptive if obedience and specific application do not take place. The purpose of the mirror is to provoke adjustment. The purpose of Scripture is to provoke obedience and produce definitive change in our lives.

Those who merely listen to the Word, Sunday after Sunday, but fail to apply the Word to their lives, will experience an increasing degree of self-deception rather than progressive sanctification. And yet isn't it interesting that they deceive only themselves? Everyone else knows full well that they are merely listening and not obeying, not maturing. It's as obvious to them as it would be if we woke up tomorrow morning, glanced in the mirror, and then walked away without ever touching the comb, the washcloth, or the toothbrush.

❝ No matter how extensive one's scriptural knowledge, how amazing one's memory, it is self-deception if that is all there is…It is not what one knows, but what one does that counts. True knowledge is the prelude to action, and it is the obedience to the word that counts in the end.[11] *❞*

— Peter Davids

So what does this have to do with this book? Small groups are not primarily intended for teaching and preaching; those functions are the responsibility of your pastor. Rather, small groups are designed for application. They create a context where Christians can apply God's truth in a personal, practical way. In order to apply God's Word effectively, though, we must first interpret it accurately.

Some groups think "Bible study" means swapping their

**Meditate on
2 Timothy 2:15.** Have
you ever been tempted
to bend the meaning of
Scripture to suit your
own purposes?

personal opinions and preferences. That's bogus. We don't gather to exchange our opinions; we gather to learn God's truth. The first step is to understand what the author's original intent was when he wrote to his original audience. Only then can we begin to apply that truth to our lives, allowing God's Word to rule over us and change us for the glory of God. (For information on a great book that details how to study Scripture, see the Recommended Reading list on page 16.)

At the heart of God's Word is the gospel of Jesus Christ. No other truth comes close to the life-changing power of the good news: God the Father has sent his only Son to live a perfect life, yet suffer the punishment for sin that we deserve, thus purchasing for us perfect and eternal forgiveness from God and acceptance by God. A small group that is committed to the Scriptures will be committed, above all else, to the gospel—committed to exploring its endless wonders, and to continually reminding one another of its centrality and unparalleled magnificence. Effective small groups are gospel-centered.

So as your small group looks into the mirror of God's Word, serious in its study of the good news of Christ crucified and risen, you should continually be making adjustments. Each year you should be able to look back and identify distinct areas in which you have changed, by God's grace, during the previous twelve months. This is the difference that participation in a gospel-centered small group is to make in our lives. This and no less.

Called to Mutual Care

In the church where I serve, we call our small groups "care groups." It's not a unique title, but it expresses a second primary purpose of small groups. Just as the first is to create a context where every member can pursue sanctification, the second is to create a context where every member can give and receive care. This principle comes straight out of Scripture:

> God has combined the members of the body and has given greater honor to the parts that lacked it, so that there should be no division in the body, but that its parts should have equal concern for each other. If one part suffers, every part suffers with it; if one part is honored, every part rejoices with it. (1Co 12:24-26)

Christians have always been characterized by their sacrificial love for each other. We are commanded to care for each other unselfishly, without favoritism. "Carry each other's burdens," Paul writes, "and in this way you will fulfill the law of Christ" (Gal 6:2).

In a Sunday-morning meeting, there are obvious limitations on our ability to express this kind of care. If I'm in the middle of a message and notice someone start to cry in the seventh row back, I can't stop preaching and go minister to that individual. I'd like to, but it wouldn't serve the entire church. In a small-group context, though, we are not so limited. Here we can both give and receive specific, personal care. No one need be overlooked or neglected.

It is important to point out that mutual care and close relationships are not dependent on the size of a church. Many assume it's impossible to form close relationships in a large church. They also assume that in a small church, close relationships will develop automatically. Both assumptions are false. Relationships can flourish in a large church…and be absent in a small one.

The ability to forge strong, personal relationships does not depend on a church's size. Rather, it depends on the doctrinal understanding and practice of the people who make up that church. Relationships will flourish in any church, no matter what size, where they are stressed as a biblical necessity.

First-time visitors to Covenant Life Church are often intimidated by its size. I can understand how they might feel this way. But as I tell them, "The longer you are involved here, the smaller this church becomes." It's a fact—over time you become more aware of the relationships you've formed than you are of the church's size. Indeed, a large church does not need to sacrifice quality relationships—but it does need to provide the small groups and service opportunities that make mutual care a reality.

Fellowship Redefined

Why small groups? A third reason is fellowship. Many small groups use this word without understanding what it really means. As a result, they aren't experiencing one of the most vital things a group has to offer. You'll look at fellowship in depth in the next chapter, so I'll try to limit myself to just a few comments on this critical topic.

Fellowship means to participate together, or to

11

communicate things we hold in common. The greatest common denominator among us as Christians is our relationship with God the Father, through God the Son, by God the Holy Spirit. This forms the content of true fellowship. Our relationship with God should be the main topic of communication within our small groups as we participate together to fulfill his purpose in the local church.

There's a catch, however. The depth of our personal relationship with God determines the degree of fellowship possible with each other. Thus, in order to know true fellowship, one must maintain a passionate relationship with and experience of God. Perhaps that is why biblical fellowship is so rare.

For Further Study:

What "litmus test" for Christian conversation do you find in Ephesians 4:29?

Fellowship is not just another word for social activities. I really enjoy watching the Washington Redskins or the University of Maryland basketball team with my friends. This can be a healthy part of small-group life…but it isn't fellowship. And you don't have fellowship talking about the latest political controversy, either. Social activities must not be equated or confused with fellowship. They are distinctly different. Nothing compares to the fellowship we enjoy when we worship together, study and apply Scripture together, encourage and correct each other, and communicate to one another our current experience of God. Nothing. Social activities can create a context for fellowship, but they are a place to begin—not a place to remain.

When I spend an extended time with another Christian, my main desire is that we experience biblical fellowship. I want to hear of his relationship with God, and how God is revealing himself to him. I want to communicate my current experience of God as well, and impart a fresh passion for God.

3 Based on the author's definition, which of these topics of conversation do you think would promote true fellowship:

O   The "one that got away" on your last fishing trip

O   The details about how you became a Christian

O   The passage of Scripture you read this morning

O   The latest site you visited on the Internet

O   Terrorism

O   The difficulties of raising a strong-willed child

O   The most recent movie you watched

Is that your desire? If someone spent an afternoon with you, would he or she leave with a fresh understanding of and passion for God?

With this definition of fellowship in mind, consider your small group. Are you experiencing fellowship? How much time do you spend in the meetings talking about your current relationship with God? When you meet together outside the meetings, how often do your conversations revolve around God's work in your life? If you are relaxing together more than you're relating together spiritually, you're not enjoying true biblical fellowship—and you have something to look forward to.

Experiencing and Expressing the Gifts of the Holy Spirit

God has given spiritual gifts to every Christian (1Co 12:1-7). He fully expects us to use them. But in a church of any size at all, it's simply not feasible for every member to use these gifts on a Sunday morning. They can in a small group, though. In this smaller and more personal context, each one can serve according to the gifting of the Holy Spirit. This is the fourth and final reason why small groups exist.

Some Christians define the Spirit's work in very narrow terms. Seminary professor Gordon Fee, who recently completed a major study of Paul's writings on the Holy Spirit, calls for a different approach. Pay close attention to this quote from his book, *God's Empowering Presence*:

> In Paul, power is not to be thought of merely in terms of the miraculous, the extraordinary...Paul understood the Spirit's power in the broadest possible way.[12]

I'm all for the miraculous and the extraordinary, but it is easy to get preoccupied with this. Our small groups need to become familiar with the varied and distinct works of the Holy Spirit. Through a combination of doctrinal study, experience, and practice, we should seek to understand the Spirit's power in "the broadest possible way."

I recommend beginning with a thorough study of Scripture concerning the person and work of the Holy Spirit. This will include seeking to define, identify, and cultivate the various gifts of the Spirit listed in 1 Corinthians 12:8-10,28; Ephesians 4:11; Romans 12:6-8; and 1 Peter 4:11. I would also recommend that you set the same goal for your group that Scripture sets: reaching the point where each member is able to serve others and glorify God with the unique gifting which has been imparted by the Spirit. Everybody should be bringing something to the party!

Let me give a few suggestions from my own experience and study of Scripture. First, in order to experience and express the gifts of the Spirit, we must develop the habit

For Further Study:
Read 1 Timothy 4:14 and 2 Timothy 1:6. What two commands does Paul give Timothy regarding his spiritual gift?

> ❝ We should make a deliberate effort at the outset of every day to recognize the person of the Holy Spirit...We should continue to walk throughout the day in a relationship of communication and communion with the Spirit mediated through our knowledge of the Word, relying upon every office of the Holy Spirit's role as counselor mentioned in the Scripture. We should acknowledge him as the illuminator of truth and of the glory of Christ. We should look to him as teacher, guide, sanctifier, giver of assurance concerning our sonship and standing before God, helper in prayer, and as the one who directs and empowers witness.[13] ❞
>
> — **Richard Lovelace**

of *communing* with the Holy Spirit. Paul ends his second letter to the Corinthian church by saying, "May the grace of the Lord Jesus Christ, and the love of God, *and the fellowship of the Holy Spirit* be with you all" (2Co 13:14). Is the fellowship of the Holy Spirit as much a reality for you as the love of the Father and the grace of Christ?

Second, we need to avoid *grieving* the Holy Spirit. I like what Jerry Bridges says on this topic:

> It is very instructive that it is in the context of interpersonal relationships that Paul wrote his warning, "And do not grieve the Holy Spirit of God" (Eph 4:30). Now, all sin grieves God, and Paul could have inserted that warning in the context of sexual immorality (Eph 5:3-5) or lying and stealing (Eph 4:25,28). But he places it in the context of sins we commit with hardly any sense of shame or guilt. The message should be clear. God is grieved over our "refined" sins just as He is grieved over sexual immorality or dishonesty. I am not suggesting that being irritable at one's spouse is as serious as something like adultery. I am saying that being irritable at one's spouse is sin, and that *all* sin grieves God and should grieve us.[14]

When we sin, we must respond quickly to the convicting presence of the Spirit; otherwise we will grieve him and break fellowship with him.

Third, we need to avoid *quenching* the Holy Spirit. In this case, the best defense is a good offense. Are we stirring up the gifts God has placed in us? When he prompts us to use them to serve others, do we obey quickly? If not, we're quenching the Spirit.

God intends for his Holy Spirit to play a central role in every church meeting, large or small. Last week's meeting is history. Tonight's meeting demands a fresh visitation by the Spirit of God. Apart from his presence, there's no point in meeting. Each of us has a responsibili-

Meditate on 1 Thessalonians 5:19.
Isn't it sobering to know that your attitudes and actions can extinguish the Spirit's activity within the group?

ty to seek the Holy Spirit and be sensitive to what he wants to accomplish in the group as we gather together. Wayne Grudem writes,

> We must recognize that these activities of the Holy Spirit are not to be taken for granted, and they do not just happen automatically among God's people. Rather, the Holy Spirit reflects the pleasure or displeasure of God with the faith and obedience—or unbelief and disobedience—of God's people…The Holy Spirit *gives stronger or weaker evidence* of the presence and blessing of God, according to our response to him.[15]

Meditate on Psalm 42:1. Here's a great verse to read on the way to your next small-group meeting.

What is *your* response to him on a daily basis? During the small-group meeting? To a degree, that response will determine the forcefulness of his presence in your midst. Let us daily commune with the Spirit and purpose to avoid grieving or quenching the Spirit, so that we can experience the full strength of his presence and pleasure.

Fourth, we should arrive at our small-group meetings *expecting* the Spirit to be powerfully present. This is essential. What a difference expectation can make as we begin our small-group meetings! It can be the difference between a life-changing encounter with God and a superficial time together with no immediate *or* eternal benefit. When each member comes expecting the Holy Spirit to reveal and refresh, together we taste the power of the age to come.

> **❝** Expectancy is a context for the gift of the Holy Spirit…People who look for something to happen are particularly candidates for the reception of the Holy Spirit…When people have expected little and expressed satisfaction with their present spiritual situation, they have received little, if anything. But those who wait to receive everything God has to give, those who desire great things from God, those who stand on tiptoes of expectation—it is they whom God delights to bless. Expect a miracle, and miracles begin to happen![16] **❞**
>
> — J. Rodman Williams

This is why we are committed to small groups. By his grace, together we are being changed into the image of Jesus Christ through progressive sanctification. Together we are experiencing mutual care, genuine fellowship, a gospel-centered focus and the ministry of the Holy Spirit. We no longer just see—we observe and understand. We no longer simply attend—we participate. We no longer selfishly consume—instead we are carrying out God's purpose for our lives as we contribute to the building of the local church.

1. How observant are you? Without looking, try to answer the following questions:

- Does this room have an overhead fan?
- What is the main image on the front of this book?
- How much money is in your wallet or purse?
- What is the brand name of the shoes you have on?
- What color are the socks/nylons of the person sitting to your left?

2. According to the author, what four goals should each small group share?

3. In simple terms, how would you describe the difference between justification and sanctification?

4. Why is the Christian life "inescapably corporate"?

5. What role do other Christians play in our progressive sanctification?

6. Do you have a Nathan—someone to whom you are accountable?

7. Share your answer to Question 2 on page 9.

8. Why might some people hesitate to share personal needs with their group?

9. Is your group experiencing consistent fellowship?

10. Is there anything you can do personally to increase the Holy Spirit's power and presence in your small-group meetings?

RECOMMENDED READING *The Discipline of Grace* by Jerry Bridges (Colorado Springs, CO: NavPress, 1994)

Let the Reader Understand: A Guide to Interpreting and Applying the Bible by Dan McCartney and Charles Clayton (Wheaton, IL: Victor Books, 1994)

How Can I Change? by C.J. Mahaney and Robin Boisvert (Gaithersburg, MD: Sovereign Grace Ministries, 1993)

The Cross-Centered Life by C.J. Mahaney (Sisters, OR: Multnomah Publishers 2002)

CHAPTER TWO

FELLOWSHIP REDISCOVERED

JOHN LOFTNESS

In the heart of Charleston, South Carolina stands an old church building. Bright stained glass offsets the solemnity of heavy red brick. Inside, pictures of Jesus and other biblical figures etched in glass filter the light of the worship place. A handcarved altar piece reaches to the vaulted ceiling. Someone gave great attention to detail in designing and building this house of worship. Above the entrance, inlaid in the brick, is a cross—the symbol and heart of Christendom for 2,000 years.

But times have changed, and the need for a house of worship has been replaced in Charleston's tourist district by the need for prime restaurant space. So today the former Church of the Redeemer has been transformed into the Mesa Grill. The church's name, carved in a marble placard at the sidewalk entrance, looks as if someone has tried to sand-blast it away. In the glass case that once announced activities and the weekly sermon, there now hangs today's menu. Where hardwood pews once filled the worship space, upholstered booths sit among potted plants. Rock music pulsates through the atmosphere; Sting has replaced Handel as nachos have replaced communion bread. None of the patrons seem particularly aware of the incongruity of the place.

> **1** Before you read further, write a definition of biblical fellowship in the space below using your own words.

Rediscovering Biblical Fellowship

As the title of this chapter announces, this is an essay about fellowship, and the Mesa Grill is an apt metaphor

For Further Study:
The Jewish Sabbath also went through a drastic change in meaning. Note the command to keep the Sabbath holy (Exodus 20:8-10). Now, see how the Jews applied that in Mark 3:1-6. Is this what God intended?

for what has happened to the practice of Christian relationship in the church today. We've kept the term and turned it into something that doesn't even vaguely represent what it means to the one who defined it.

Fellowship is like that old church building. People have started using the term to describe ways of relating never intended for this precious communion of the saints. And because God created the practice, we'd better make sure we use it in the way he designed it–because God isn't putting fellowship up for sale. Remember what happened when Jesus found the Temple being used as a place to turn a profit?

What fellowship is not. In its neglect, Christians have redefined fellowship to mean any warm human interchange—especially when we make connection with someone and discover that we have common interests, experiences, or viewpoints. I enjoy the outdoors. Hiking, canoeing, and fishing are among my favorite leisure activities. When I meet someone who knows the joys of the Rose River Trail in Shenandoah National Park, or has canoed the rapids of the lower Youghegheny River, or thrills at the first yank of the line signaling the strike of a smallmouth bass, our conversation is inevitably animated and friendly. But it is not fellowship.

If I spend time with a brother in Christ playing volleyball, talking about shared political views, or following the ups and downs of an NFL franchise, we may have a wonderful time and deepen a friendship. But in none of those things will we have had fellowship.

Let me press the point further. Fellowship is not (at least not necessarily) going to a Bible study with someone, or sharing doctrinal commitments, or attending a Christian men's rally where emotions run deep and passions are high. Fellowship is not found in a "group therapy" session where participants reveal their darkest thoughts—even if everyone in the group is a Christian and brings a Bible. In fact, two Christians can be married to one another and still not experience fellowship.

I have heard Christians complain that their relationships seem superficial and they don't know why. What they often fail to see is that, while all Christians have relationships, not all relationships include fellowship. In fellowship, God offers us a precious but neglected gift—a type of human relationship created exclusively for his children. If God thinks it's that important, we had better find out what it is.

18

For Further Study:
Even if you have
neglected biblical
fellowship, God can
restore what you have
lost—a principal seen
in Joel 2:25.

What fellowship is. Fellowship is a uniquely Christian relational experience. No one but those born of the Spirit of God can have fellowship—which makes its neglect all the more tragic.

The word "fellowship," as it is found in the English Bible, is a translation of the Greek word *koinonia*. Saying the word aloud brings to mind our word "community," and so it should, for *koinonia* is its root. But sadly, politicians and sociologists have effectively redefined "community" to mean "special-interest group," so we need additional words to get at its meaning. Here the Revised Standard Version of the Scriptures can help. It translates *koinonia* as "fellowship," but also as "participation," and "sharing" (in the following verses, these words are italicized for emphasis).

And they devoted themselves to the apostles' teaching and *fellowship*, to the breaking of bread and the prayers (Ac 2:42).

So if there is any encouragement in Christ, any incentive of love, any *participation* in the Spirit, any affection and sympathy... (Php 2:1).

...and I pray that the *sharing* of your faith may promote the knowledge of all the good that is ours in Christ (Phm 1:6).

What is fellowship as defined in the New Testament? Just this: participating together in the life and truth made possible by the Holy Spirit through our union with Christ. Fellowship is sharing something in common on the deepest possible level of human relationship—our experience of God himself.

Participating together... life and truth...sharing in common...human relationship...experience of God—these phrases capture the essence of the unique Christian experience of fellowship. Opportunities to fall in love, get mar-

---

**MEMORABLE MOMENTS
IN SMALL-GROUP HISTORY**

A last-minute phone call informed me our musician couldn't attend the small-group meeting that evening. I grabbed a CD of worship songs as we went out the door to go to the meeting.

When I put on the CD, soft music drew some people directly into worship. Their eyes closed, they lifted their hands, expressing tender love toward God. Others, however, were breaking into fits of laughter. I thought the Holy Spirit had fallen on the group. But the musical interlude was way too long. It suddenly dawned on me that at home we'd mixed up our CDs and cases, and that for the past few minutes some of us had been worshiping to *John Tesh Live At Red Rocks*.

— **Mario Stemberger (Holly Hill, FL)**

ried, procreate, pursue a career, go bungee jumping, play baseball, or go to school are all open to humanity in general. But only Christians can experience fellowship. For this reason alone, this unique quality of Christian existence should be exceedingly precious to us. We should eagerly explore its meaning so that we can fully mine its treasure. My sincere hope is that this chapter will compel you to seek a deeper experience of fellowship.

Start with God

Fellowship with God is the prerequisite to fellowship with others. This is the explicit message of John in his first biblical letter:

> We proclaim to you what we have seen and heard, so that you also may have fellowship with us. And our fellowship is with the Father and with his Son, Jesus Christ....If we claim to have fellowship with him yet walk in the darkness, we lie and do not live by the truth. But if we walk in the light, as he is in the light, we have fellowship with one another, and the blood of Jesus, his Son, purifies us from all sin (1Jn 1:3, 6-7).

The flow of John's argument may not be as straightforward as modern readers prefer, but his logic is clear. John and his fellow teachers (the "we" of the passage) have come to know truth through the life and teaching of Jesus. This has allowed them to have fellowship with God the Father and with the ascended Christ. This fellowship exists not only *with* God but *between* and *among* those who "live by the truth." Sin ("walking in darkness") not only pollutes our fellowship with God but hinders our fellowship with one another. "Walking in the light"—obeying God's word and confessing our sins when we disobey—should result in fellowship.

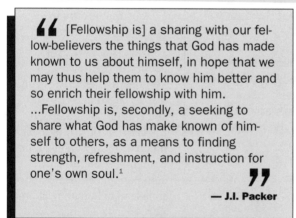

" [Fellowship is] a sharing with our fellow-believers the things that God has made known to us about himself, in hope that we may thus help them to know him better and so enrich their fellowship with him. ...Fellowship is, secondly, a seeking to share what God has make known of himself to others, as a means to finding strength, refreshment, and instruction for one's own soul.[1]

— J.I. Packer

In short, fellowship with others begins with an honest, open, obedient relationship with God rooted in the truth of his Word. *How we share that relationship with oth-*

ers—how we wrestle with understanding truth and struggle to apply it to our lives—is the essence of fellowship.

Thus, fellowship has one source and two channels. The one source is God. The two channels—both to be understood in the light of Scripture—are the work of the Spirit directly in our hearts, and the work of the Spirit through other believers.

Some, upon hearing this, might be tempted to get off the bus that takes them to fellowship. Relationships, even between believers, come packaged with problems. To pursue relationships is to open ourselves to hurt, misunderstanding, and inconvenience, for our relationships are inevitably influenced by our sin.

You may think fellowship with God is all you need. After all, doesn't the Bible teach that God and his Word are sufficient for all our needs pertaining to life and godliness? Yes, it does. But the error comes in limiting the means God uses to help us apply truth to our lives. Only the Spirit can illuminate Scripture to our minds and give us the power to obey it. *Yet the Spirit often chooses to employ other people as a means of communicating his truth to our ears and heart.* Who are we to argue with him? He will of course use teachers of the word through sermons, books, and tapes. But he will also use the regular guy in your small group—and there's the rub. We can ignore teachers, close books, and turn off tapes. When we do pay attention, we can conveniently misapply teachings. But the people closest to us, if they're doing their job in fellowship, are not likely to let us ignore God's urgings so easily.

We're like the Israelites trudging through the wilderness, like the disciples huddled in the upper room after Jesus' ascension, like the pilgrims on the Mayflower. The negative view is that we're stuck with one another—confined by a desert, a hostile Jerusalem, or a stormy sea. But "stuck" is not the biblical attitude. Rather, we *belong* to one another. We are pilgrims on our way to the promised land, called to help one another along on the journey. God has chosen fellowship to be a primary channel of life in his body.

For Further Study:
Read Psalm 15:1-2; 51:6. How important are honesty and truthfulness to maintaining a right relationship with God?

2 Have you used any of these common techniques to try to "turn off" God's voice?

❑ The Technical Foul: Presuming that God will never speak to you through anyone who is not at a specific level of maturity and holiness.

❑ The World's Oldest Excuse (see Genesis 3:11-13): Presuming that, if several people are involved in some sin, then what you did is somehow less serious than if you had acted alone.

❑ The Jonah Method: Running away from God's direction in your life because you think you might not like the outcome.

❑ The Peter Problem (see Mark 14:27-31,66-72): Placing more faith in what you say about your strengths than in what God says about your weaknesses.

Meditate on Romans 12:5. What does it mean to belong to one another?

The Means of Fellowship

Ever heard the phrase "a means of grace"? In theology, it refers to things we can do—such as pray or meditate on Scripture—to put ourselves in a position to receive something from God. Fellowship is a means of grace, too. It's a way of getting to a place where God will meet us. So the next question is: what are the means of *fellowship*? What can we do to posture ourselves to experience fellowship? The list is long.

Worship God together. Worship is a means of experiencing fellowship with God through meditating upon and declaring truth about him, giving thanks to him, and receiving a sense of his presence. As we noted earlier from Scripture, fellowship with God—including worship—opens us to fellowship with one another.

Pray for one another, especially regarding the things that burden us and how God is at work in our lives. Praying together is about as close as we can get to experiencing someone else's fellowship with God and knowing the qualities of his relationship with his Lord.

Utilize our spiritual gifts to help others grow in God. If fellowship is participating together in the Spirit, what more obvious participation can there be than to serve one another through those grace-gifts empowered by the Spirit?

Carry one another's burdens. Paul puts it this way: "Brothers, if someone is caught in a sin, you who are spiritual should restore him gently. But watch yourself, or you also may be tempted. Carry each other's burdens, and in this way you will fulfill the law of Christ" (Gal 6:1-2). We all have burdens and—as I once heard my pastor, C.J. Mahaney, say—we have a responsibility to communicate those burdens without requiring anyone to receive divine revelation in order to know what they are. But this process does not have to be difficult.

> **❝** Those first Christians of Acts 2 were not devoting themselves to social activities but to a relationship—a relationship that consisted of sharing together the very life of God through the indwelling of the Holy Spirit. They understood that they had entered this relationship by faith in Jesus Christ, not by joining an organization. And they realized that their fellowship with God logically brought them into fellowship with one another. Through their union with Christ they were formed into a spiritually organic *community*.... We must grasp the idea that fellowship means belonging to one another in the Body of Christ, along with all the privileges and responsibilities that such a relationship entails.[2] **❞**
>
> — **Jerry Bridges**

22

HOUSE RULES FOR GOD'S FAMILY

1. Be at peace with each other (Mk 9:50)
2. Love one another (Jn 13:34)
3. Be joined to one another (Ro 12:5)
4. Be devoted to one another (Ro 12:10)
5. Honor one another (Ro 12:10)
6. Rejoice with one another (Ro 12:15)
7. Weep with one another (Ro 12:15)
8. Live in harmony with one another (Ro 12:16)
9. Accept one another (Ro 15:7)
10. Counsel one another (Ro 15:14)
11. Greet one another (Ro 16:16)
12. Agree with each other (1 Co 1:10)
13. Wait for one another (1Co 11:33)
14. Care for one another (1Co 12:25)
15. Serve one another (Gal 5:13)
16. Carry one another's burdens (Gal 6:2)
17. Be kind to one another (Eph 4:32)
18. Forgive one another (Eph 4:32)
19. Submit to one another (Eph 5:21)
20. Bear with one another (Col 3:13)
21. Teach, admonish each other (Col 3:16)
22. Encourage one another (1Th 5:11)
23. Build up one another (1Th 5:11)
24. Spur one another on (Heb 10:24)
25. Offer hospitality to one another (1Pe 4:9)
26. Minister gifts to one another (1Pe 4:10)
27. Be humble toward one another (1Pe 5:5)
28. Confess your sins to one another (Jas 5:16)
29. Pray for one another (Jas 5:16)
30. Fellowship with one another (1Jn 1:7)

One day I was sitting in a church office as four of us on staff concluded a business meeting. As we got up to leave, I simply said, "I need to let you guys know what is going on in my heart." That's all it took to get the process underway.

Less than a month earlier we had buried an eight-year-old boy who had died of cancer. Matt had been more than a church member; he was a friend to me and my family. I had been feeling a heaviness—a sadness—since then, and I wasn't sure its source was pure, or that I was handling it correctly. Though it seems obvious now, I couldn't tell what was going on in my heart.

My friends listened quietly as I groped to explain myself. But they didn't just comfort me. They asked probing questions surrounding issues of self-pity, worry, and a prideful sense of responsibility. It took courage to ask such questions of someone struggling with the sadness I faced, but those questions needed asking, and I didn't know enough at the time to ask them of myself.

When my friends were done, I knew someone understood me—and not just in an emotional sense. They had helped me explore my soul. Their counsel? Watch out for certain temptations, but mainly, you're grieving, John. The sadness you feel is a normal part of the painful losses we experience in life.

For Further Study:
Read Job 2:11-13.
When we try to counsel
or comfort someone, is
it always best to get
right to the point?

Did my sadness leave on that day? Did I walk out of that office on clouds of joy? No. But three other men were now carrying my burden, and I left with a much lighter load.

We need to communicate the burdens of our *trials*. Not just the external challenges of losing a job or enduring an illness, but the inner conflicts as well. We also need to communicate the burdens of our *fears*, which are often embarrassing but can rule our souls. What a tragedy when the burdens of Christians weigh them down because they neglected to receive help through fellowship!

Share about our spiritual experiences. Since she was in high school my wife Nancy has kept a journal of her times alone seeking God. It's not unusual for her to read to me from it, and I share the same sorts of things with her. It often just takes five minutes, but it's rich fellowship just the same.

Confess our sins to one another—before someone comes to confront us. This obvious source of help in conquering sin is often neglected because of our foolish pride. "Therefore confess your sins to one another," James writes, "and pray for each other so that you may be healed. The prayer of a righteous man is powerful and effective" (Jas 5:16).

Correct one another when we see someone has failed to recognize and take responsibility for his sins. Paul writes that when we see a brother caught in a sin, we should point it out to him to help promote his restoration (Gal 6:1). As uncomfortable as this is, *it is fellowship*. And if we are at first unsuccessful in winning the errant brother, Jesus teaches us to widen the circle of fellowship to ensure the correction is accurate and the brother receives every chance to be won (Mt 18:15ff).

Correction (see Chapter Five) is one of the more challenging aspects of fellowship because it often entails disagreement and conflict. Moreover, the one bringing correction may end up having his own motives evaluated—and found wanting. Yet without this dynamic of fellowship, we wall up portions of our lives, blocking us from other opportunities for fellowship.

Serve one another in practical ways. Effective serving requires knowing another's needs. Discovering these needs is often the product of fellowship. Imagine that a couple in your group reveals that they are experiencing unusual conflict due to neglect of their marriage. Fellowship may mean taking their children for a weekend so the parents can get away and work on righting the wrongs of their relationship.

We must, however, beware of thinking that the mere act of doing of any of these things will automatically produce fellowship. Remember, these are "means of fellowship." They simply put you in a place where fellowship becomes *possible*, not certain. True fellowship is a work of the Spirit by grace. And as with the Tango: it takes two to fellowship, and not everyone wants to dance. Still, failure to practice these *means of fellowship* denies us the opportunity to draw on fellowship as a *means of grace*.

Hindrances to Fellowship

In an essay on fellowship J.I. Packer identifies four hindrances to enjoying this particular dynamic of life in the Spirit: self-sufficiency, formality, bitterness, and elitism.[3]

Self-sufficiency. This sin announces to God and others that we are adequate in ourselves. It reveals itself in a lack of prayer (demonstrating our delusion that we don't need God) and a lack of fellowship (demonstrating our delusion that we don't need each other).

For the past 30 years Christians have been fascinated by 1 Corinthians 12 and the other New Testament passages about spiritual gifts. Often, the underlying question has been, "What are my gifts?" If our concern is for serving, this is a good question. But taking a broader view of the chapter reveals another issue: *We need each other*, for different people have different gifts. To say that we can become who God wants us to be without benefit of fellowship is as inaccurate as saying that a body can be fully functional without eyes or hands or ears.

In our self-sufficiency we tend to ignore fellowship—only to discover our need for it when we hit a crisis. Then we scramble to build relationships just when we have the least time for them, and when people—for good reason, given our history—have concluded we have no interest in fellowship.

Formality. The word can conjure images of debutante balls and trying to remember which fork to use. But here all it means is those rules and standards we unconsciously employ when we're in social settings. Sometimes these rules are neutral, but sometimes they inhibit fellowship. Consider the unwritten code of some families: "You don't talk about your 'private' life with other people." You won't produce much fellowship taking *that* belief into the church!

3 Do you have any habits or heart attitudes that keep you from growing in Christ through fellowship? How about these?

❏ Because of my heritage, I'm naturally stoic and reserved, so I tend to keep to myself.

❏ I tried that kind of fellowship once, and I gave a whole lot more than I got, so I tend to keep to myself.

❏ I was an only child, so I tend to keep to myself.

❏ My brothers and sisters were the ones always clamoring for attention, so I tend to keep to myself.

❏ Maybe I'll go along with this fellowship stuff, as long as somebody else goes first.

We can also fall into formality within our small groups—the very place where fellowship demands spontaneity and openness. In fact, I've found the meetings of many small groups to be as predictable as any liturgy (and I say this without any intent to denigrate congregations that employ a liturgy). The leader follows a standard pattern. The same people pray, read Scripture, talk about their problems. Every time.

But fellowship is spiritual—"of the Spirit"—and so should our meetings be. The needs and issues of our lives change, and so should the content and topics of our meetings, for the Spirit is constantly at work in our lives to conform us to Christ's image in specific ways. We must adapt to his work, and invite others to help us. I'm not advocating there be no plan or format to meetings, but rather, that the plans include opportunities for everyone to share the work of the Spirit in his or her life.

Bitterness. Bitterness in the context of fellowship is

simply a sinful reaction to something gone awry in a relationship. Consider these areas:

For Further Study:
Why did Joseph's brothers plot to kill him? What had gone wrong in their relationship? (see Genesis 37)

- Unfulfilled expectations: "I've invited him to lunch, and he didn't accept; I've opened my life to him and he didn't follow up; I thought we would become close friends, but instead he spends all his time with someone else."
- Offended pride: "Your correction was inaccurate, and I'm insulted that you'd even think I could do such a thing. I'll never open my life to you again."
- Jealousy: "Why is he the group leader? Can't the pastors see that I'm far more talented?"
- Gossip and slander. Telling someone privileged, negative information about another when the recipient is neither part of the problem nor part of the solution—this is gossip. Slander, which is the spreading of false information about someone with an intent to harm him or her, tempts those slandered to grow bitter. Left unconfronted, gossip and slander create mistrust and bitterness, building a wall of hostility fellowship cannot scale. Worse yet, these sins tend to create factions within the group, which only separate believers further from one another.

Elitism. This condescending attitude toward those whom we deem less mature than ourselves quenches fellowship—or turns it into a narrow one-way street. We find elitism in this kind of thinking: "I can help him, but he's not mature enough to make any contribution to *my* growth. I only share my life with people mature enough to handle my problems." Or we can form cliques rooted in the pride of tenure: "I've been here a long time and my relationships are established. Those folks would probably be more comfortable with some of the newer members."

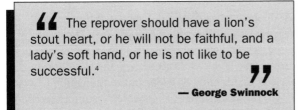

> The reprover should have a lion's stout heart, or he will not be faithful, and a lady's soft hand, or he is not like to be successful.[4]
>
> — **George Swinnock**

Getting from Here to There

Ask. Once we are committed to the value of fellowship, creating opportunities for it is quite simple. Ask people questions that go beyond the superficial. Get past "How're

ya' doing?" to "How is God working in your life right now?"
"How did that event affect you?" "What do you think you
can learn from this?"

We seem to find it much harder to *ask* such questions
than to answer them. Most of us desire to share our trials,
burdens, successes and interests with others—all we lack
is a brother or sister with a willing ear.

Volunteer. Fellowship flows when we volunteer information about our internal state to others *not simply to
relieve the problem of loneliness, but to gain their honest
evaluation of how we are dealing with the issue and how
we can change.* Correction is rarely given unless we invite
it. Recently a friend asked to speak to me privately. He
was struggling with temptation toward a besetting sin,
and his appeal was memorable: "I appreciate your support
when I confess my trial and sinful reaction, but I need
more than your understanding and support. I need you to
rebuke me in *strong terms*. Please get my attention by
correcting me in strength." This man enjoys deep fellowship, and his growth in God has been consistent partly
because he recognizes his need for help, and he knows the
Spirit uses others to provide insight.

Take advantage of ready-made opportunities. I prepare
for my small group with two things in mind: first, what
issue in my life is God bringing to my attention—a sin or
temptation, a trial, an opportunity or decision, confusion
over some issue. I come ready and willing to open my life
and receive input on this issue. As a practical matter, we
can't always get to everyone, so we may not cover my issue
that evening, but I'm ready if we do. (And if we don't, I look
for other opportunities.) Second, I approach the meeting
recalling past issues others have brought up so I can
express my care and encourage fellowship by following up.

My group meets in two settings: as couples (all of us
are married), and separately as groups of men and
women. We use discernment as to which issues are appropriate for the mixed group and which demand discretion.

Be creative. Other opportunities for fellowship abound.
Hospitality is a biblical practice that fosters fellowship.
Conversation tends to flow freely during a meal, whether
it's in someone's kitchen or at a restaurant. Parties can
also help create fellowship—if we make room for it.

Go camping together. Room near each other at the
church retreat. Any contact between Christians—especially those in your own church, and most especially those in
your small groups—should be seen as an opportunity for
fellowship.

For Further Study:
Read Titus 1:12-13.
What motivated Paul to
use strong correction in
specific cases?

For Further Study:
Read Romans 12:13
and 1 Peter 4:9. Is
hospitality recommended,
or commanded?

All in the Family

One of the metaphors by which Scripture describes the church is the family. There is much concern today about the family. Society as a whole has been alarmed to discover that individual families, and even the institution of the family, grow weak if they are not nurtured (the trendy term is "dysfunctional"). With all the discussion of such families, one might conclude they are the only kind left.

But that's far from true. There are lots of healthy, "functional" families. Of these, I'm convinced the best ones are found in biblically based Christian homes that have their roots planted deep in the soil of the local church.

The Biblical word for family is usually translated "household," and when we become Christians, we become members of God's household, his family. Look at three passages from Paul:

> Therefore, as we have opportunity, let us do good to all people, especially to those who belong to the family of believers (Gal 6:10).

> Consequently, you are no longer foreigners and aliens, but fellow citizens with God's people and members of God's household (Eph 2:19).

> If I am delayed, you will know how people ought to conduct themselves in God's household, which is the church of the living God, the pillar and foundation of the truth (1Ti 3:15).

4 Think of the best family you have ever known. Now, write down three things about that family that made it so good.

1)

2)

3)

Are there truths here that can be applied to your church?

Each of us has family responsibilities in the church. Fellowship encompasses a major responsibility to care for another's soul and to get help for our own so that together we can be all that God intends us to be.

A good local church—and a good small group—is like the best of families. Good families take responsibility for each other. Good families are honest with each other. Good families take care of each other. Good families deal with their problems. Good families love each other—no one is lonely. Good families love and respect the head of the household—in our case the one we call Father and Lord.

Fellowship makes family life possible in the church.

But fellowship doesn't happen of itself. We must define it, we must pursue it, we must love it. If we do, we will prevent someone from turning our spiritual household into a restaurant. ■

GROUP DISCUSSION
1. Read the definition of fellowship you wrote in answer to Question 1 on page 17. Do you still think that's the best definition? Why or why not?

2. Can you name an activity you once believed to be fellowship, but which actually is not?

3. Which spiritual gifts do you think you may possess? (see Romans 12) How might these promote fellowship in your small group?

4. Do the members of your small group know about any of the spiritual experiences that have made the greatest impact in your life?

5. Self-sufficiency, formality, bitterness, elitism: Do these categories suggest any areas of sin you may need to confess? Invite the evaluation of others.

6. Take a poll. Do most people in your small group find it easier to *answer* a question about their spiritual life than to *ask* such a question of someone else?

7. If the answer to Question 6 is yes, then go ahead and ask someone about his or her spiritual life—because most people won't mind answering!

8. Pray that God would help you have the humility and passion to seize future opportunities for fellowship.

RECOMMENDED READING *The Crisis of Caring* by Jerry Bridges (Phillipsburg, NJ: Presbyterian and Reformed, 1985)

CHAPTER THREE

TAKE THIS GROUP AND OWN IT!

GREG SOMERVILLE

W e begin with a tale of two cars: an aging Plymouth Voyager and a sleek new Lincoln Continental. I had the opportunity to drive them both last year, but I treated them quite differently.

The Plymouth minivan looked as if it had been owned and operated by a second-rate day care center. There were footprints on the vinyl and nose prints on the windows. Cracker crumbs littered the floor. Acorns, rocks, chewing-gum wrappers, and other collector's items filled the cup holders. In the cracks between the seats I found a wide assortment of archeological remains. And judging by the smell, the windows had been left down during a series of heavy thunderstorms.

It was a well-used vehicle.

The Lincoln, on the other hand, appeared to have rolled off the assembly line moments before I got behind the wheel. The floor mats were *not* sticky with spilled soda. The rearview mirror had *not* been knocked off and reattached three times. The carpet didn't ooze with some unidentifiable engine fluid. The odometer had not broken a thousand, much less a hundred thousand. And the smell—is it only guys who notice?—the smell of that new leather interior, untainted by rotten bananas and car sick-ness and all the other fragrances of a family van.

It was a beautiful car…but it was a rental car, and I treated it that way. I filled it up with low-grade gas. I accelerated fast and braked hard. I didn't wash it, vacuum it, or change the oil. And by the time I returned it to the rental lot, those pristine floor mats were thick with dirt and sand.

My Plymouth Voyager isn't much to look at, but it's mine. (And it's paid for!) I wash it, change the oil, check the tire pressure, and vacuum it out when the cracker crumbs get too deep. This morning I dropped it off at the body shop, hoping the skilled staff at Paintmasters can unbend a fender that just got smashed. My vehicle looks worse than ever, but it's mine. The rental car wasn't. And that explains why I treat an aging minivan better than I treated that mint-condition Lincoln Continental.

The issue is ownership. Not only does ownership affect the way we care for our cars and homes and lawns, but it determines how much—or how little—we invest in our small groups.

**Meditate on
1 Timothy 4:12-15.**
Why did Timothy need this encouragement? Do Paul's words motivate you to contribute more actively in your group?

Do you think of your group as *your* group?

Do you *own* your group and its vision?

Or do you simply rent a chair on Thursday evenings?

As a group leader, I usually don't have to think about these questions. Of course I'm an owner. I'm supposed to lead by example in worship, in prayer, in discussion, and in fellowship. If I simply show up and smile, there's a good chance the meeting will be a flop. (Though God is gracious enough to spare even the most incompetent leader!)

Recently, though, my friend Jim has been leading our discussions. This has given him a great opportunity to grow in leadership…and given me a great opportunity to fine-tune my laziness. Suddenly it doesn't seem so essential that I study the book in advance. The pressure isn't on me to think up questions that will help others apply what we are learning. During this season, Jim is the one having to discern where the Spirit is leading our discussion—not I. So guess who has tried skimming the material 30 minutes before the meeting? That's right. As a result, I not only neglect to feed my own soul, but I lower the quality of my contributions to group discussion.

If you see yourself as an owner of your group, you will take the assignments seriously. You will show up on time. You will work to make the group a success. But if you're only renting space you won't be motivated to invest yourself. You may go along for the ride, but when the group hits a pothole or some maintenance is required, you may choose to look for a new group rather than get under the hood and help make repairs.

Your group may not be a new Lincoln Continental. It may be an '86 Ford Escort with bald tires and a leaky radiator. But it's yours! And you're responsible for taking care of it. Look closely at Paul's words to the church in Ephesus: "From him the whole body, joined and held together by every supporting ligament, grows and builds itself up in love, *as each part does its work*" (Eph 4:16).

A small group doesn't belong to the leader. It belongs

to God—and to each member. Each member is an owner. Each member is equally responsible for insuring that the group glorifies God. And unless God calls you to a different group, you have the privilege of making this one run as well as it can.

Everybody Has a Job

My next-door neighbor has the nicest lawn on our street. He has owned his property for over 30 years, and now that he's retired, he spends a lot of his time making it beautiful. The guy who lives across the street, however, is a different story. When his wife's car is blocking the driveway, he simply drives his truck across the yard. The big ruts in the lawn don't bother him. Why? Because he's a renter and knows he'll eventually be moving out. Someone else will have the responsibility of re-seeding the lawn. It's not his job.

In a small group, everybody has a job. That's why the pastors in my church have written a "Small-Group Member Job Description" (see page 37). It explains what is expected of each member. As you read, notice that it assumes a high degree of ownership.

Did you realize your job was so big? It's critical! "No member of the church should be isolated or uninvolved," writes Brent Detwiler. "Only through your enthusiastic involvement will the church be able to do everything God has called you to."[1]

Meditate on 1 Corinthians 12:7.

Why does God give you the "manifestation of the Spirit"?

What is the greatest need for improvement in your group right now? How can you help?

What Makes a Group Successful?

Suppose R.C. Sproul taught your small group, Larnelle Harris led worship, Billy Graham oversaw evangelistic outreach, and Mother Teresa coordinated your service projects. Wouldn't that be fantastic? Can you imagine the potential your group would have?

Actually, by my definition, the group would almost certainly fail. For in the shadow of such gifted leaders, you would be tempted to leave ministry to the "experts" and neglect your own responsibility. And small groups don't succeed unless the entire group is working together.

It doesn't take a highly gifted leader to build a great group. But it does take men and women who are devoted to applying Scripture, to practicing fellowship, to serving their church, and to sharing the Gospel.

Peter expresses the essence of Christian community—and of small groups—in these compelling verses:

The end of all things is near. Therefore be clear-minded and self-controlled so that you can pray. Above all, love each other deeply, because love covers over a multitude of sins. Offer hospitality to one another without grumbling. Each one should use whatever gift he has received to serve others, faithfully administering God's grace in its various forms. If anyone speaks, he should do it as one speaking the very words of God. If anyone serves, he should do it with the strength God provides, so that in all things God may be praised through Jesus Christ. To him be the glory and the power for ever and ever. Amen. (1Pe 4:7-10)

For Further Study:
Read 1 Corinthians 12:14-20. God has given us all unique parts to play in our groups. Do you know what *your* part is?

For more than seven years I've enjoyed the privilege of leading a group who live by the principles in this passage. These men and women discipline themselves to pray. They love each other deeply. They freely extend hospitality. Best of all, they serve each other with the gifts and grace God has given them. Not perfectly, of course—we all have plenty of room to grow. But through their faithful and creative service in the church and community, they are bringing much praise to God.

Your small-group leader may never teach at the seminary level. Your worship leader probably won't release his own CD anytime soon. But in God's eyes, your group can be a total success...here's how.

Hunger to know God. The single greatest contribution you can make to a group is your own passionate pursuit of God. This is true for two reasons.

As you diligently study God's Word, pray, worship, confess sin, witness to non-Christians, and cultivate the various expressions of a healthy Christian faith, your zeal will influence the entire group. Your passion will spur others on "toward love and good deeds" (Heb 10:24). Do you realize that your example can accomplish more than a month's worth of teaching and exhortations from the leader? You are the proof that a passionate life is possible...and not just for leaders.

> **"** In a typical church, 20 percent of the people do 80 percent of the work. Thankfully, this has not been my experience. What a joy it is to serve with people who are giving their lives away in service—people who are committed to using their gifts and graces in the context of the local church.[2] **"**
>
> — **Brent Detwiler**

Secondly, as you press in to a deeper knowledge of God, he will reveal himself to you. He will give you fresh insights about his fatherly love, or understanding of his holiness. But these aren't just for your benefit. They are also for the group. As you mine the riches of God's grace and kindness and share your discoveries with the group, you'll find they are enriched as well.

Love the church. Sooner or later, your group leader (or another member) will do something you don't like. Probably it will be minor—an unpleasant assignment or inconvenient request. But if it's major, what's going to keep you from seeking "greener pastures"?

Meditate on Ephesians 5:25-27. What does this passage tell you about God's love for the church?

Suppose your leader asks you to reach out to a new member of the group—someone from another culture with a thick accent and different customs. Suppose he challenges you to fast for a couple of days, or participate in a pro-life march, or spend a Saturday helping with a church service project. What if another member of the group confronts you (and not very tactfully) about the way your children behaved at the group picnic?

You will find it easier to respond if you genuinely love the church, its leaders, and the priority they place on small groups. Jesus gladly laid down his life for the church. To make your group a success, be prepared to lay down some things as well. It may be uncomfortable; it may force you to do something you've never done. But for

2 Genuine love is sacrificial love. Can you think of one thing you have done in the past month that would indicate you love the church?

the sake of Christ and his church, give it your best.

Understand your "job description." I think it's safe to speculate that most small-group members have clear expectations of their leader but vague (or nonexistent) expectations of themselves. They have never understood, or embraced, their role as co-owners in the group. As a result, the group never comes near its potential—even if it has an outstanding leader.

The sidebar on the next page lists the expectations my church has of small-group members. As you can see, it's quite specific—and quite challenging! Your church may not define small-group membership the way my church has, but this kind of "job description" is invaluable. Find out what your pastor expects of group members in your church, and then begin doing your job!

Assume your leader is *not* Sherlock Holmes. How I wish I had this venerable detective's gift! It would serve me (and the group) so well if I could take one look at a couple and say, "Ah, yes...Marital Conflict #174—He thought he was serving the family by bringing home pizza (observe the sliver of pepperoni under his left thumbnail), and she broke down sobbing. Why? Note the calculator sticking out of her purse—she's convinced he is wasting the family's money and leading them straight into bankruptcy. Elementary, my dear Watson. Here's all you need to do...."

Your leader would like this type of discernment, too, but I doubt he has it. Don't make him guess how you're doing, what you're feeling, when you're struggling. Please don't doubt his concern just because he can't read your mind. He wants to be involved, but he needs you to tell him *when* and *how*.

Sometimes you have to tell a leader twice...or more. If I kicked myself for every time I've failed to follow up when a group member asked for my input, I would be black and blue. When you've shared a need, and the leader has apparently forgotten all about it, don't retreat into a sinful shell of self-pity. Share it again. Muster up the courage to be vulnerable. God will give you grace as you humble yourself.

Share the bad stuff, too. One of the best ways to make

For Further Study:
What character trait is absolutely essential in order for you to confess sin to others? (Read 1 Peter 5:5)

> ### Job Description
> #### SMALL-GROUP MEMBER
>
> **Purpose:**
> To apply God's Word and develop relationships for the purpose of maturity, service, and outreach.
>
> **Qualifications:**
> - Membership in the church and a commitment to its leadership, mission, and ministry
> - Ability to participate in the group without disrupting or monopolizing the time and attention of the group (Serious issues should be referred to a pastor)
>
> **Spiritual Goals:**
> - Consistent devotional life
> - Specific application of God's Word in daily life
> - Growing relationships with spouse and children (if applicable)
> - Growing relationships with other small-group members
> - Meaningful service in the church through use of spiritual gifts
> - Involvement in friendship evangelism
>
> **Personal Responsibilities:**
> - Participate in all functions of the corporate church and ministry sphere
> - Arrive on time for all small-group meetings, service projects, social events, and outreach functions
> - Complete assignments and come to meetings prepared to participate
> - Build meaningful relationships with other members of the group outside scheduled meetings
> - Open one's life to others by being honest, transparent, and teachable
> - Support the leadership of the small-group leader

your group successful is to confess your own sins. Just last week, two women in my group shared specific details about sins they were battling. What an impact it made! Long after we have forgotten the material we studied that night (which was about overcoming sin), our group will remember the confessions these ladies gave. They demonstrated what we were discussing. They brought the lesson to life.

An honest confession can break a superficial meeting wide open. Be humble. Be honest. On the other hand, be wise—certain confessions should be shared privately, or in single-sex groups.

"Confession begins in sorrow," writes Richard Foster, "but it ends in joy. There is celebration in the forgiveness of sins because it results in a genuinely changed life."[3] Not only will you receive God's grace as you confess sin, but the whole group will be provoked.

Have realistic expectations. One of these days you are going to realize that your group leader has problems, just like you. Maybe he's not as knowledgeable about the Bible as you are. He may not appear especially passionate or gifted. As a result, you may find it difficult to follow or respect his leadership. But ultimately the problem stems from your expectations, not his qualifications.

> ❝ A man who confesses his sins in the presence of a brother knows that he is no longer alone with himself; he experiences the presence of God in the reality of the other person. As long as I am by myself in the confession of my sins everything remains in the dark, but in the presence of a brother the sin has to be brought into the light.[4] ❞
>
> — **Dietrich Bonhoeffer**

Your group leader isn't your pastor. No one expects him to be. His main purpose is to create a context where group members can apply God's Word and care *for each other*. Understand his role and you will find it easier to accept his limitations.

Meet outside the meeting. A few members of my small group have had the audacity to get together *outside our meetings*. Apparently they think they can grow relationally apart from my leadership. I plan to squelch this practice, of course, as soon as I find out who is doing it. But the group is getting so tightly knit together that I'm not sure anyone will confess!

Open your home. You may not have the biggest or nicest home in the group, but offer to host meetings, outreaches, or times of hospitality. By opening your home, you open yourself...and you drive another nail into pride's coffin. If your home *is* the nicest in the group, you may face other temptations to avoid hospitality—especially if the group includes dozens of kids! Remember that the early Christians "had everything in common" (Ac 2:44)—even if that meant the first-century equivalent of ice cream spills on the rug or kids' fingerprints on the walls.

Open your mouth! Some need little encouragement here. They should probably skip this suggestion. But in the group I lead, people are so polite and humble and self-controlled...it can be *very quiet* at times. Sometimes wisdom keeps us quiet (Pr 17:28). More often than not, pride (disguised as fear or shyness) is the real culprit. It is pride that tells us we should only speak when we have a profound insight or wonderful testimony. Yet often the Holy Spirit will use your simple, honest comment to speak directly to someone's heart. Don't let pride deprive the whole group of your valuable contributions.

Meditate on Proverbs 29:25. What is the snare described here? How might it keep you from speaking out in a group context?

Be constructive, not destructive. Weeks before I went off to college, I learned I would be rooming with that year's national debate champion. I quickly resolved that I would do my best to avoid getting into arguments with this guy. And it paid off.

Most groups include at least one member who has a knack for twisting discussions into debates. In his letter to Titus, Paul warns against those who engage in "unprof-

3 In some cases, it would be wrong for you not to respond to a controversial statement. Are any of the following in that category?

❏ "My work just doesn't allow time for these meetings."

❏ "Would God really expect me to love a spouse like mine?"

❏ "I'm having a hard time trusting God in this situation."

❏ "This is the most pitiful group I have ever attended."

❏ "Doesn't the pastor seem to lack vision for the church?"

❏ "I refuse to trust a God who sends sinners to hell."

itable and useless" controversies and arguments (Tit 3:9). You may be the type who enjoys a good debate, and that's great—at the right time. But when small-group discussions heat up, use your gift of communication to help the leader resolve the issues. Look for ways to help others recognize and apply biblical truth.

Laugh at the leader's jokes. This is absolutely essential. However, it may not be easy. Your leader's timing, delivery, and sense of humor may be so poor that laughing would violate your sense of integrity. In that case, I recommend that you invest in a laugh-track tape. Hiding a cassette player under a couch generally works well. Just make sure you don't turn it on by accident while someone is weeping in response to conviction of sin....

Serve on the "advisory committee." Every member has the responsibility to give the leader feedback and suggestions. Remember: this is *your* group, not just his. What are its strengths? How could it improve? Do you know of a book or tape series that might benefit the whole group? Is the leader giving enough direction? Too much? Does it seem a bit excessive to have the group meet seven nights a week? Share your thoughts with the leader, then trust his decisions. He may not do cartwheels over your first idea, but don't give up. Keep bringing suggestions. He will appreciate it.

Pray on the way. As you drive to the meeting, instead of doing what you typically do on the way to your small group—argue with your spouse, or think about unresolved problems at work, or try to guess what weird questions the Dorkenschmidts will ask tonight—why not pray? Ask God to send his Holy Spirit in power. Ask him to direct your leader. Ask him to bless the other members. And ask him to help you participate

---

MEMORABLE MOMENTS IN SMALL-GROUP HISTORY

One night I was leading a discussion that was so dynamic, the guy sitting next to me fell asleep...with his head flopped on my shoulder.

I let him stay there for a while, figuring that sleep was probably more beneficial to him than my teaching.

— **Mickey Connolly (Charlotte, NC)**

enthusiastically in worship. I can almost guarantee that a few minutes of prayer on the way will revolutionize your gatherings.

Once you have that mastered, consider praying for the group on a more regular basis. I try to pray for each member of my group several times a week. Do you know what happens when I do that? I get insights on how I can serve or encourage them. Best of all, my affection for them deepens as I labor with them in prayer. It may not seem like much, but your intercession for the group will produce great results.

Give your gifts. Let's look again at that passage from Peter's first epistle:

> Each one should use whatever gift he has received to serve others, faithfully administering God's grace in its various forms. If anyone speaks, he should do it as one speaking the very words of God. If anyone serves, he should do it with the strength God provides, so that in all things God may be praised through Jesus Christ. (1Pe 4:10-11)

Whether you realize it or not, God has given you at least one spiritual gift. Maybe you have a gift of giving, or faith, or mercy. Your talents may lie in the area of music or administration. (The New Testament gives lists of spiritual gifts in Romans 12, 1 Corinthians 12, and Ephesians 4.) Regardless of the gift, it comes from God, and it's been given to you for a purpose—to serve others and glorify God. Here are a few guidelines for using these gifts in a way that pleases the Giver:

Be humble. We need to avoid the twin pitfalls of pride: self-consciousness and self-exaltation. Recently, a woman in my group shared a beautiful prophecy urging us to embrace God's purpose during the "rain" of life's hardships. It affected everyone present. But as she confessed later, she almost didn't share it with the group because she was afraid of what others might think. What a loss that would have been! Three years from now, if she keeps exercising and refining this gift, she could possibly slide to the other end of the spectrum and assume that her gift gives her higher spiritual status. That form of pride would also grieve the Spirit. To administer God's grace faithfully through spiritual gifts, we need a special blend of boldness and humility.

Be faithful. If you practice using your gift, it will increase and grow stronger. If you stop using a gift, it tends to shrivel up. This principle is clearly taught in

Meditate on Ephesians 6:18.
Paul's command here is not very subtle...do you get the hint?

For Further Study:
Read 1 Corinthians 3:5-8. Though we must be faithful in the use of our gifts, who makes them *fruitful*?

Matthew 25. Remember the story of the servants and the talents? Jesus praised the two servants who doubled their money through faithful investing, but he strongly rebuked the servant who buried his money in the ground. That story should sober us all. We must invest God's gifts with care.

Be dependent. To serve God and others effectively with these gifts, we must "do it with the strength God provides." You may not feel you have much to offer the group...and you're absolutely right! *But God does*, and he wants to do it through you. Not only do the gifts come from him, but so do the strength and skill to administer those gifts "so that the body of Christ may be built up" (Eph 4:12).

Your small group provides the ideal context for you to practice using your God-given gifts. Think about specific ways you can invest and increase them. Get suggestions from your group leader. Ask God to give you more so that you can, in turn, give more to the group. Whether he has called you to prophecy or hospitality or exhortation or serving, begin utilizing your gifts here.

Volunteer to serve. Who is in charge of refreshments? Who keeps track of birthdays? Who makes phone calls to announce a change in the meeting schedule? Who administrates the outreaches? Who relays information to the members who missed the meeting? The leader who has to do all these things himself won't have time to lead. Help him—and the whole group—by taking some of these tasks yourself.

One small-group leader in my church developed a list of service opportunities within the group, complete with job descriptions for each. You may want to set aside a meeting to talk about ways to divide up the "chores." As the group becomes more and more fruitful, you'll have the joy of knowing that you helped make it happen.

> **❝** There is no other way to grow in anything apart from constant practice and risking. The only good athlete you will ever see is a bad one who didn't give up. The only good disciple you will ever see is a bad one who didn't give up...If we don't risk, our gift will not grow, and if our gift does not grow, the Lord will not be pleased with us.[5] **❞**
>
> **— Jack Deere**

4 Below is a list of common needs within small groups. Check any of these you currently do, and circle those you could possibly do in the future.

❑ Coordinate refreshments

❑ Keep a group prayer log

❑ Supervise child care

❑ Host meetings

❑ Lead worship

❑ Lead discussion

❑ Organize outreaches

❑ Make phone calls

❑ Other_____

Expect "awe-full" meetings. In the fourth chapter of Acts, we read of a rather significant small-group meeting. Peter and John had just been interrogated by the Jewish leaders, who commanded them to stop preaching in the name of Jesus. After boldly dismissing their threats, Peter and John returned to where the other disciples were meeting in an upper room. They gave a full report and then the believers prayed. Did they ask God to protect them, to shield them from persecution? No—they prayed that God would make them even bolder! And Scripture tells us the results: "After they prayed, the place where they were meeting was shaken. And they were all filled with the Holy Spirit and spoke the word of God boldly" (Ac 4:31).

I am not suggesting that every successful small-group meeting has to end with an earthquake. But we must realize the potential that exists when we gather. The same Lord who shook that upper room and shook off the chains of death is in our midst!

Meditate on Matthew 18:20. Here is one visitor who should always feel welcome in your meetings!

If you're more excited about the coffee and brownies than about being with God, something is very wrong. Raise your expectations! Stir up your spirit in anticipation of God's powerful presence. Expect to see the Holy Spirit working actively in your midst.

Keep the mission in mind. I find it sobering that my small group is the size of most church-planting teams... or bigger. When I hear of a church-planting team being sent out, I fully expect it to multiply until it has made a lasting impact on the city it has targeted. Do I have similar expectations of my small group? The gifting may not be as great, but we should be able to make a mark on our neighborhoods for Jesus Christ.

God is responsible for building his church, and he is using small groups effectively for that purpose. He could have chosen to do all the work himself. But instead he has created a structure in which you play a pivotal role.

It doesn't take a highly gifted leader to build a great group. It takes you. You must own it. You must pray for it and invest in it. Whether you feel qualified or not, you and every other group member must "use whatever gift he has received to serve others, faithfully administering God's grace in its various forms" (1Pe 4:10). As you humble yourself, apply yourself, and give yourself to God and those he has placed around you, you will have the joy of making your small group a success. ∎

GROUP DISCUSSION

1. If your group were an automobile, what kind would it be? A new Porsche? A 12-year old minivan? A Humvee? Something else?

2. A home owner is expected to do things like mow the lawn and trim the hedges. What types of responsibilities do you think a *small-group owner* should have?

3. Before reading this chapter, did you think the group leader was responsible for the group's success?

4. Read 1 Peter 4:7-10. What might happen if you tried to serve your group *without* the strength God provides?

5. Did any items in the job description on page 37 surprise you?

6. The greatest contribution you can make to your group, says the author, is your own pursuit of God. How would you rate your passion for God at this time? (1=ice cold, 10=red hot)

7. Would you be willing to confess a sin in the context of this group? If not, why?

8. Name one thing this group does really well.

9. Do you expect God to participate powerfully in group meetings?

10. In what ways do you think the group could improve?

RECOMMENDED READING

Life Together by Dietrich Bonhoeffer (San Francisco, CA: Harper & Row, 1954)

The Mark of the Christian by Francis Schaeffer (Downers Grove, IL: InterVarsity Press, 1970)

CHAPTER FOUR

WHAT MAKES A GREAT LEADER?

MARK MULLERY

The golf course was right where the freeway should have been. I would normally enjoy finding myself at a golf course, but not under these particular circumstances. You see, my wife Lesley and I had been visiting a friend and gotten lost driving home. We didn't have a map. The more we wandered around the countryside, the darker it got. After enough wrong turns to frighten our children, we finally found the missing freeway (maybe somebody had moved it), and headed for home—way behind schedule.

So it goes when you've lost your way: tensions rise, time is wasted. Leading small groups really isn't very different. In order to be effective, the group must have a clear direction. More specifically, the *leader* must have a clear direction. And whether you are a group leader or one of the members, it's essential that you understand what the position of leadership involves.

Let's Start at the Beginning...

What is the small-group leader's purpose? As you look back on a meeting—or a year's worth of meetings—how will you know if you've been successful? What do your pastors want the group to accomplish? Without a clear understanding of its purpose, your small group will wander here and there without any sense of mission.

In our church, one thing we've done to avoid such aimlessness is to set forth a clear definition. Our small-group leaders are in place...

to extend the pastoral ministry of our church...

by providing a context...

in which to apply God's Word...

so that growth, care, and relationships may occur.

Every component of this definition is significant, so let's look at each of them in turn.

To extend pastoral ministry. Scripture teaches that churches are like flocks of sheep with shepherds to watch over them. These shepherds, also known as pastors, are charged by God to lead, feed, and care for the people God entrusts to them. In all but the smallest churches, this immense task is too difficult for one or even a few people. Moses found this out when he tried single-handedly to solve the problems of a few million Israelites during their 40-year trek through the wilderness.

Moses' father-in-law Jethro came and counseled him,

> What you are doing is not good. You and these people who come to you will only wear yourselves out... select capable men from all the people—men who fear God, trustworthy men who hate dishonest gain— and appoint them as officials over thousands, hundreds, fifties and tens. Have them serve as judges for the people at all times, but have them bring every difficult case to you; the simple cases they can decide themselves...If you do this and God so commands, you will be able to stand the strain, and all these people will go home satisfied (Ex 18:17-23).

By Jethro's insight, which constitutes a primary biblical definition of leadership, Moses learned how to provide the Israelites with superior care, and live longer himself in the process!

It is God's design that every pastor identify and train trustworthy men who fear God, investing them with real authority and responsibility to extend the pastoral ministry of the church. As Moses learned (and New Testament examples show the same), this is done most effectively through small groups. Small groups serve a local church immeasurably by bringing each member into ongoing relationships with trained and gifted small-group leaders who can serve and equip them in many ways. In this manner, the pastors are better able to concentrate on the ministry of God's Word and equipping others for ministry.

However, pastors should never become disconnected, and they should remain available to deal with the diffi-

Meditate on Romans 15:14. Though pastors should handle difficult counseling needs, is it necessary to take every problem directly to the pastor?

1 In your opinion, which of the following problems are so serious that they should be handled by a pastor rather than a small-group leader?

❏ My husband watches four hours of television every night and never talks to me.

❏ I often find myself cursing at lousy drivers who won't get out of my way.

❏ Why can't I find the Book of Hezekiah in my Bible? I know it's here somewhere!

❏ I have never had a consistent prayer life.

❏ My cat is stuck in a tree.

cult issues as they arise. That availability releases the small-group leaders from any false notions that they are now expected to function as pastors. Their job is to *represent* the pastors, not *replace* them.

By providing a context. Recently, I was in a restaurant with a menu featuring beautiful, glossy, full-color pictures of chocolate milk shakes. I like chocolate milk shakes. I was psyched. When it came my turn to order, the waitress said—to my surprise—that she was unable to serve me a milk shake.

Now, in this restaurant there was milk, ice cream, chocolate syrup, and a hungry customer—every ingredient necessary for the sale and thankful consumption of a chocolate milk shake. Unfortunately for me, there was no way to bring all these elements together. The milk shake machine was broken.

Church life can be like this. You can have great preaching and teaching, trained leaders, and hungry Christians. But if you don't have a context where all the elements can be combined, you face disappointment.

Sunday meetings are obviously great times for God's Word to be preached, but where and how will the Word be applied? Sunday meetings are great places for people to come together, but how will these people move from being mere acquaintances to becoming accountable to one another? Sunday meetings present great opportunities for the ministry of the Spirit but, logistically, how can everyone exercise their unique, God-given gifts? It just wouldn't work.

> 66 Union with Christ necessarily involves union with his people. The church is not simply a 'means of grace,' useful to our growth; it is a necessary part of Christian experience, to be taken with utmost seriousness.[1] 99
>
> — Bruce Milne

Small groups provide an excellent context in which to pursue many of the vital goals of church life that are difficult, if not impossible, to pursue on Sunday mornings. And the small-group leader provides an invaluable service to the church by facilitating that process.

To apply God's Word. The Bible is our guide for faith and practice. Only the Bible teaches what God requires of us and what we must believe about God. No other book is sufficient to equip us with all we need to live by God's grace and for God's glory. Accordingly, small groups in the church I serve are built around God's Word. The members often use meetings to explore more deeply the teaching they receive on Sunday mornings. For Christ to be formed in us we must apprehend God's truth and then apply it to our lives. Therefore our groups often feature discussions that help us to understand God's Word and apply it practically to our daily lives.

So that growth, care, and relationships may occur. There are lots of small groups meeting these days. From Alcoholics Anonymous to your local chapter of Hell's Angels, folks gather for a variety of reasons. Scripture provides three good reasons to gather in small groups: to promote sanctification, to extend care, and to develop true fellowship. Small groups aren't the only places in the life of the church where growth, care, and relationships are furthered, but they are vital ones. They provide a context in which God's Word can be applied personally and practically, where friendships can blossom and grow, and where non-christians can experience something of the life of God's people. This truth affects our definition of what makes for an effective small-group leader.

Success in leading a small group isn't measured by how many are in the group, how fast it grows numerically, or how frequently it meets, but by whether the members of the group are increasingly dying to sin and living to righteousness. A great small group is not one where people are wowed by the Bible knowledge of the leader, but one where people take a genuine interest in the lives of others in the group. A model meeting isn't one that goes on for three hours because the leader lets the discussion range across a dozen topics, but one that ends with members confessing sins and applying biblical truth to everyday areas of their lives.

Four Easy Ways to Ruin a Small Group

Failure in leadership isn't difficult. For most of us it comes rather naturally. So here, with tongue planted firmly in cheek, are a few proven suggestions that will enable you to ruin your group in record time:

Tip #1: Do it all yourself. Training others is hard work. It takes time. Frequently those upstarts don't do things exactly the way you would, which of course is totally unacceptable. They might even try new things! Plus, asking people to help out can be intimidating. So wouldn't it be easier just to do it all yourself? If this doesn't work, here's another suggestion: do nothing at all! Save your preparation for the last minute...so it'll be fresh! Skim the reading while you comb your hair; work out discussion questions in your mind during worship. Nobody will know the difference.

Tip #2: Strive to become a self-contained mini-church. Small groups can be a great outlet for the ambitious but frustrated leader. Instead of seeing yourself as part of a team—working in concert with other small groups to glorify God by fulfilling the vision God has given your pastors—imagine yourself as the only one who really understands God's will and direction for your group. Make every effort to build into the group members a unique loyalty to you and your personal style of leadership. Keep yourself (your special charm and wisdom) at the center of everything that happens. Try to make your group self-sufficient so people won't feel the need to participate in other aspects of church life. One great way to do this is to plan so many events that people are always busy doing group-related things. It's especially effective to set up events that overlap with other church-wide events, causing members to have to choose pretty regularly between, say, a camping trip with your group and the church's Sunday meeting.

Tip #3: Have all the answers. During discussions, you as a leader can easily ruin a meeting by showing off your extensive knowledge of biblical, theological, historical, and sports trivia. When someone poses a question, jump right on it so everyone can be impressed with your keen mind. (If you wait too long, somebody else might take a shot at it and an actual discussion might ensue!) Above all, try to keep the meetings in an "ask the expert" format. They should hang on your every word. If you don't know the answer to a question, never let on. Just finesse it. Two effective approaches are either to insinuate it was a dumb question in the first place, or re-direct the question so that someone else is embarrassed rather than you.

Tip #4: Go easy on the encouragement. As everyone knows, encouragement brings life into a meeting like springtime brings flowers. That's why you want to avoid it at all costs. One effective strategy is to remain so focused on yourself and your "performance" as leader that you simply don't notice anyone else. Another is to set up so many rules, guidelines, and expectations that no one can

For Further Study:
Read James 3:13-16. What can a leader expect to reap if he is selfishly ambitious?

2 One of the best aspects of small-group involvement is knowing that you are serving your local church. Here are four questions to make sure that is the case:

	Yes	No
Do you know your pastor's goals and guidelines for the group?	❑	❑
Do you seek your pastor's advice when making long-range plans for the group?	❑	❑
Are your group activities and outreaches designed with the church in mind?	❑	❑
Does your group involvement reinforce your involvement in the church?	❑	❑

Meditate on 1 Thessalonians 5:11.
Can you think of *one thing* to say to *one person* at your next group meeting that would build him or her up?

possibly *deserve* encouragement. Perhaps best of all, make time to point out people's faults and shortcomings, while overlooking the grace of God in their lives. If you do, I can guarantee you that failure is just around the corner.

Certainly there are many more ways to wreck a good small group. I trust the comic approach used here is a helpful reminder that God has invested leaders with a great deal of responsibility. Though you are not expected to replace the pastor, you do represent him, and your behavior will have more influence on the life of the group than anyone else's. This awareness should motivate you to deepen your foundation in God's grace, put to death the sin that still dwells in you, and cling tightly to the Holy Spirit who alone can give you the power to know God and die to sin. Further, in your role as leader you will set the pace for your group in humility. Be honest and vulnerable about your struggles and sins, and aggressively seek out evaluation both from your group and your pastor. Try asking these people, "How can I serve you better?"

MEMORABLE MOMENTS IN SMALL-GROUP HISTORY

I had been a small-group leader just two months when our meeting fell on Halloween night. A man in our group had been reaching out to his neighbor, a Catholic. Just before the meeting was to start, Tom called me. He said he couldn't come because he wasn't feeling well. But he'd seen his neighbor and she was on her way...dressed in a devil's costume.

She showed up in red—trident, tail, hood with horns—the works. I tried to head her off at the door. "That's an interesting costume," I began, "but we don't celebrate Halloween...."

"Oh, that's OK," she said, walking right past me. "I thought I'd come as Martin Luther, since he was a devil from hell."

Though we didn't rise to the bait—and continued our meeting as if nothing were out of the ordinary—this episode did put a damper on our outreach for a while.

— **Gerard Snyder (Brookhaven, PA)**

Qualifications for a Small-Group Leader

There was a time in our church when we had people leading small groups before they had been in the church long enough to become members. Later, as the pendulum swung back the other way, we believed the qualifications for a small-group leader were virtually the same as those for a pastor.

Somewhere in the middle are reasonable qualifications that fulfill the spirit of Exodus 18:21 (capable, trustworthy men who fear God and hate dishonest gain), Acts 6:3 (men from among you known to be full of the Spirit and wisdom), and 1 Timothy 3:8-10 (sincere men, worthy of respect, not indulging in much wine nor pursuing dishonest gain, keeping hold of the deep truths of the faith with a clear conscience, tested with nothing found against them). In the church which I serve, we have come up with the following ten qualifications for small-group leaders:

Committed. An effective leader is wholeheartedly committed to *his* church, *his* pastors, and the goals they hold for that church. This means recognizing that God's hand has sovereignly brought him into *that* church and into leadership *there*. This gives him a platform of faith from which to support, encourage, and represent his church leaders. A leader who has caught this vision will pass on to his small group the same values, doctrines, and emphases his pastor would if he were there personally. He will seek to strengthen the group's commitment to the Lord, the local church, and their pastor(s) rather than to himself. Such a leader will actively seek to direct the people in his group into the ways of God and the unique expressions of God's grace operating in that church.

> **❝** Leadership is not a title that grants you license to force others to knuckle under; it's a skill you perform, a service you render for the whole group.[2] **❞**
>
> — **Fred Smith**

Of proven character. When Moses or the apostles went looking for men to serve in key positions, they sought out those who were "among them" with proven character. Clearly, men must be tested before assuming a leadership role. They must not be made leaders unless and until they have demonstrated sufficient character. If this principle is ignored, God's name will be maligned as leaders are exposed in various sins. *Character is imperative*—a non-negotiable. The ability to gather a crowd, demonstrate powerful spiritual gifts, speak eloquently, lead dynamic discussions or worship—none of these are sufficient for biblical leadership. Significant character must also be present. We're not looking for sinless perfection, but the potential leader should display the fruit of the Spirit, growing humility, a consistent ability to manage his time and responsibilities, as well as sufficient maturity to care for his own soul and still have enough grace left over to care for others.

Submitted. The Greek verb "to submit" (*hypotasso*) is a combination of two words. One means "under" and the other means "to put someone or something in charge." Together they mean "to put under someone or something in charge." Thus, the leader who wishes to be effective

For Further Study:
Read John 5:19. Jesus knew he could "do nothing" on his own; he was totally submitted to his Father's will. Do you exhibit the same type of submission to authority?

3 If you are serving as a small-group leader, rate your responses to each of the following questions.

How did you respond to your former leader?

←——————————————————→

Submitted   **Not Submitted**

When your pastor gives you instruction, do you listen carefully and follow through?

←——————————————————→

Submitted   **Not Submitted**

When the Holy Spirit convicts you of sin, do you resist or embrace his correction?

←——————————————————→

Submitted   **Not Submitted**

At work, would your boss describe you as respectful, easy to lead, and eager to see others succeed?

←——————————————————→

Submitted   **Not Submitted**

must understand both authority and submission—he must acknowledge that being *in* authority depends on his willingness to be *under* authority. As a citizen he is "under" the governing authorities (Ro 13:1); as a Christian he is "under" God's authority (Jas 4:7); as a church member he is "under" the authority of his church leaders (1Co 16:16); if a husband he is "over" his wife (Eph 5:23); if a father he is "over" his children (Eph 6:1); at work he may be "over" certain employees (Eph 6:5). Jesus marvelled at the faith of the centurion who, because he understood himself as a man both in authority and under authority, was actively yielded to the authority of Christ (Mt 8:5-10).

If you are leading a group now or perhaps aspire to lead a group in the future, don't dismiss this question: Are you submitted to authority? Are you a good follower?

Having a love for people. As already noted, leading a small group means serving as an extension of the pastors in the shepherding of the church. It is essential that the man who takes this position have a growing love toward the people for whom he cares. The Bible describes as a "hired hand" the man who looks after sheep—and is thus technically a shepherd—but whose sole motivation is personal gain (Jn 10:11-13). While the small-group leaders in our church definitely couldn't be motivated by the income they receive from us (long hours, no pay!), there are many selfish and ungodly reasons that might motivate someone to lead a group. An effective leader must be motivated by love for God's people and a sincere desire to serve them as they are conformed to the image of Christ. This love will be reflected in the way he prays for them, supports them through trials, and encourages them, as well as by the way he corrects, admonishes, and instructs them when appropriate.

In a commendable mar-

❝ Most people judge the counsel they receive by the way they receive the affection of their counselor. See that you feel a tender love for your people, and then let them feel it by your speeches and see it in your dealings with them...Let them see that all you do is for their own sakes and not for your own end.[3] **❞**

— Richard Baxter

riage (if applicable). It's not hard to imagine why a man with a bad marriage would be disqualified to lead a small group. He's going to have some difficulty holding the group's respect if, as he is urging them to read the assignment, she pipes up, "Put your money where your mouth is, slick! You haven't read any of the last three assignments and you know it!"

Simply put, leadership begins at home. Anyone who is not leading his own wife into the ways of God's wisdom and grace is simply not qualified to lead a group—and he certainly shouldn't be encouraged to export his failures into the lives of others!

Trained. As we discussed earlier, the small-group leader's goal is to promote sanctification, care, and fellowship in his group. Specific training is generally needed to accomplish this. Training topics should include the purpose and practice of small groups in your church, as well as practical skills such as leading discussions, worshiping in small groups, time management, delegation, training new leaders, and so on. Further, each leader should receive training in basic and essential doctrines such as justification and sanctification.

Consistent in the spiritual disciplines. A leader must already be what he calls others to become. If he is calling others onward and upward in God, he must also be pressing ahead himself. Consistently practicing the spiritual disciplines not only helps make the leader a worthy model for others, it provides fuel for his own fire. How will he bring truth to his group if he isn't immersing himself daily in the only book that faithfully contains God's revelation of truth to man? With what will he feed his group if he hasn't been with God? How can he sense the leading of the Holy Spirit if he isn't cultivating a relationship with the person of the Holy Spirit? If his soul is not refreshed, how will he refresh others? And what else will refresh his soul but time in the presence of his Maker?

Able to lead. While character, training, love for people, and the like are all essential for the leader, so too is the gift of leadership. However, it is easy to overestimate the need for this gift. The small-group leader is not a "mini-pastor" who must spend 15 hours preparing a discussion, nor must he be able to counsel people through the most difficult crises. Still, he must be *able* to lead. People must be willing to follow him. He must know how to make decisions in a way neither dictatorial nor democratic. He must be able to sense the leading of the Spirit. He must have the self-control and discipline necessary to steer a

Meditate on Psalm 78:72. Wouldn't you like to be led by someone with these virtues? David's skill in leading his people didn't just happen. He let God and others train him.

For Further Study. Read Romans 12:6-8. According to this passage, what is ultimately required for effective leadership?

4 Which of the following seems like the best way to show someone a sin or character flaw?

❑ During group discussion ask, "Is anyone else fed up with the fact that Bill here always lies to everybody?"

❑ During worship on Sunday, pass the following note to Mary: "Thus saith the Lord, if you leave the building to smoke a cigarette, I'll send fire down from heaven."

❑ Invite Randall over for dinner and tell him he can't have dessert until he repents of gluttony.

❑ After prayer and searching the Scriptures, ask Sarah when would be a good time to discuss what seems to be an area of sin in her life.

❑ Anonymously mail Jake photocopied pages from your Bible with applicable verses underlined in red.

discussion in a profitable direction and keep the group on course. He must have the courage to show group members their faults, and the wisdom to know when and how to do this. These are some of the things embodied in the gift of leadership—a gift which surely can be cultivated and developed, but which must be present just the same.

A tither. Not much need to explain this qualification. How we spend our money reveals our priorities. A man's commitment to tithing reveals much about how he views God and his church. Would you want a man who wasn't tithing to have the responsibility of leading your group?

Male. By now it has probably become apparent that we are assuming the small-group leader ought to be a man. This is our understanding of Scripture, though we believe it is appropriate for a woman to lead a small group consisting exclusively of other women (Tit 2:1-5).

For some, male-only leadership may be a point of dispute or consternation. We live in a day when women are finding increasing opportunities, both in the church and the marketplace, to take on roles traditionally held by men. However, our conviction on this point does not derive from culturally prevailing views, but from the sound and clear teaching of Scripture.

Men and women have much in common. Both are created in God's image (Ge 1:27). Both have inherited a fallen human nature (Ge 3:22-24). As believers, both may receive the benefits of salvation (Gal 3:26-29); share the expectation of full redemption in the day of Christ Jesus; enjoy equal access to God through their mediator Christ Jesus; know the joy of the filling of the Holy Spirit; and find fulfillment in being stewards of the Gospel. Yet standing alongside these equally shared benefits are clear biblical teachings which affirm the significant and wondrous distinctions in their roles and functions.

The God-breathed words of Scripture reveal that men and women are distinct in their masculinity and femininity. These distinctions were designed by God, are established in creation, and were affirmed by the Apostles (1Ti

2:11-14; 1Pe 3:1-7). These fundamental differences between men and women are not culturally derived. More significantly, they are not a result of the fall. At creation, God made Adam the leader and head in his relationship with Eve (Ge 2:18-24). Even before the effects of sin, Eve was divinely given the privilege of glorifying God by being Adam's helper.

Men and women are equal in God's sight as bearers of his image, but we have been given differing levels of authority. This is not a concept that Bible-believing Christians of any era should find difficult, for we see the same relationship modeled in the Trinity: the Son joyfully submits to the will of his co-equal, the Father; and the Spirit is sent by both the Father and the Son.

It is God's design that the complementary differences between men and women be evident in the home and church. In the church, governing and teaching roles are specifically reserved for men. Leading a small group is one such role because it involves oversight—caring for people, counseling them, and providing a sense of direction.

To some, these convictions may seem restrictive and wrong. From our experience, however, they release women to fulfill their God-given roles and functions. We trust that small groups who study these passages of Scripture will, in the words of Wayne Grudem, "discover true biblical manhood and womanhood in all of their noble dignity and joyful complementarity, as God created them to be, and will thus reflect more fully the image of God in their lives."[4]

WHAT ABOUT THE SMALL-GROUP LEADER'S WIFE?

A small-group leader's wife should support her husband by using her spiritual gifts to promote spiritual growth, care, and fellowship in the group. She should exhibit the same character qualities as her husband, including a consistent practice of the spiritual disciplines, commitment to the church, and love for people. However, her actual duties will vary based on her gifts, strengths, season of life, and time constraints. She is not the co-leader, nor should she feel the burden of that responsibility. Each leader's wife will function in different ways, yet each will demonstrate a commitment to serve the group in whatever ways she and her husband find appropriate.

For Further Study. For an example of differing roles in the Trinity, see 1 Corinthians 8:6; for an example of the Father's authority over Jesus, see Luke 22:42.

How to Have Dynamic Discussions

What makes for a great small-group meeting? Leaders, here are several tips. You want to provide a pleasant, clean environment for the meeting itself. Having a greeter assigned to welcome people can help create a warm and friendly atmosphere, especially for guests. The spiritual depth and musical quality of your worship times may not rival what you normally experience on Sunday mornings, but if you keep the focus on God and his amazing grace, profitable worship times can be had even with *no* instruments or gifted singers. Encourage your group to eagerly desire spiritual gifts, especially the gift of prophecy which can uniquely bring God's comfort, encouragement, and strength. Times of ministry and prayer for one another are a vital aspect of the meeting; these might take place during worship or after a discussion.

One part of the meeting that requires especially strong leadership skills is discussion. Let's look closely at four steps that will assist you in leading effective discussions.

Keep in mind that the goal is to apply God's Word. This is what your group is all about—the working out of God's Word in the daily lives of your group's members. You must remain committed to this purpose. If you don't, discussions will gradually drift into being mere debates, story-telling times, or sessions of "can you top this?" Even when the discussion material is from an article or book, the leader's goal should remains unchanged: highlight the biblical truth in what the author is saying. Only Scripture is useful for teaching, rebuking, and correcting so that God's people may be equipped for every good work (2Ti 3:16-17).

Bring good questions. Developing good questions is hard work. Even if you've been provided a list of questions, there is still much to be done. A leader must carefully work through the meeting material in advance (i.e., more than 30 minutes before the meeting starts!). Consider the people in your group. What topics would best serve them? What truths about God ought to be brought out? Pray and ask the Spirit of God to guide you into truth that will benefit your group. This is not some religious formality, but part of our ongoing communication with and reliance on God.

Good questions cause people to interact with the material and apply it to their lives. A helpful pattern is to have the discussion begin with observation, proceed to interpretation, and end with application.

Observation: *"What are the facts?"* For example: What details does the author mention? What are the key words or ideas?

Interpretation: *"What do the facts mean?"* For example: What is the author trying to say to the people to whom he is writing? Why did he write this? What is the main point? How would you summarize the author's purpose?

The goal of interpretation is simple and yet critical: to understand what the author intended to communicate to his original audience. A great deal of today's Christian study materials routinely ignore "original intent," and instead directs readers to focus on what the biblical text means to them—an approach we should categorically reject. Professor Walt Russell has written a brilliant article revealing the pitfalls of "what-it-means-to-me" interpretation. We have reprinted it as an appendix at the end of this book—don't miss it!

Application: *"What am I going to do about it?"* For example: Why do you think we studied this material? What does this material tell us about God? What does it tell us about ourselves? How do you think God wants your life to be affected by this information? What is something you plan to do differently as a result of this?

During the discussion, keep your goals in mind. When I lead a discussion, I desire that several things happen. I want everyone to participate. This means I must rein in talkative folks and gently draw out the quiet ones. As the discussion moves on, I keep in front of me the questions I've prepared and the critical points I've planned to cover. This helps me notice when we start "chasing rabbits" instead of moving in a productive direction. While holding on to my original plan, I also strive throughout the discussion to be sensitive to the leading of the Spirit, ready to adjust or change course when appropriate. Sometimes a seemingly trivial comment by a group member exposes the tip of an iceberg, and a sensitive response on my part may serve the person by giving him or her an opportunity to open up further.

Press to application. *The most challenging aspect of leading a discussion is trying to press the point home to application.* The leader who fails to bring application leads his group down a merry path into deception! James teaches us that merely listening to God's Word without doing what it says is self-deception (Jas 1:22). We think *knowing more about* God is the same thing as *being more like* him. Wrong! Information alone is insufficient. Transformation is required. (Demons know sound doctrine but remain unchanged by it.) We must respond. We must apply. By the power of the Spirit and for the glory of God, we must change. Indwelling sin is at work in our flesh, but we must put it to death. The imputed righteousness we received from Christ at the Cross must now, by God's grace, pro-

For Further Study:
Read Proverbs 19:24. Can you imagine a more pitiful picture of having a truth at your fingertips (so to speak), but failing to apply it?

gressively become a functional holiness reflected in our thoughts, intentions, values, habits, decisions, actions, and words. What better place to do this than a small group? What better time than in response to a discussion centered around God's Word?

Leading and Motivating by Grace

In 1985 an earthquake struck central Mexico, bringing destruction to a wide area. The intensity of the huge quake—8.1 on the Richter scale—was greatly magnified in Mexico City because the metropolis had been built on a dry lake bed. When the earth began to shake, the soft ground beneath the city liquefied, amplifying the effects of the temblors. The absence of bedrock below ground greatly increased the devastation above ground.

> **❝** Your worst days are never so bad that you are beyond the *reach* of God's grace. And your best days are never so good that you are beyond the *need* of God's grace.[5] **❞**
>
> — **Jerry Bridges**

The life of the Christian is designed to be built on the bedrock of God's grace. You were saved by grace alone. You are being sanctified and changed by grace alone. You will be received into glory by grace alone. The basis for your relationship with God was, is, and ever shall be *sola gratia,* grace alone! A capable small-group leader will be sure his life and his group are both solidly fixed on the Rock—the person and saving work of Christ our Lord.

Are you growing in grace? Here are some questions you can use to check your "grace meter":

- Are you more aware of what Christ did for you at the Cross than what you have (or haven't) done for him lately?
- Are your weaknesses a point of discouragement or a place where you find God's strength?
- When you haven't properly prepared for a meeting, do you expect the worst?
- After a meeting, are you painfully aware of how things could have been changed or improved?
- Can you laugh at yourself?
- Are you quicker to notice a group member's spiritual growth, or his or her faults?
- After a good meeting, do you feel God is more pleased with you than after a bad one?
- Do you avoid trying new ideas for fear of failure?

Meditate on Ephesians 2:8-9.
Don't ever, ever forget the wonderful truth found in these two verses!

- When you have prepared well, do you feel you deserve a unique measure of God's presence and power in your meeting?
- Is the Cross a central focus in your meetings?
- Does your group have a growing confidence in God's sovereignty, holiness, and grace?
- Are your meetings characterized by joy or rules?

A small-group leader occupies a unique and vital role in the church. He serves the church's leaders by extending their ministry. He serves his group by providing a context where, by applying God's Word, they can grow in holiness, give and receive care, and develop godly relationships. He serves his God by growing in grace while pointing others there as well. ■

GROUP DISCUSSION

1. In a single sentence, write down what you think is the purpose of this group, then compare your answers.

2. Why is a small group such a great context for growth?

3. What were your answers to Question 2 on page 49?

4. How well is your leader running your group? Rate him on a scale of 1 (no damage) to 10 (total devastation).

5. Why do you think the author placed such an emphasis on *applying* God's Word?

6. Here's your chance to lead by humble example, fearless leader: In which of the ten qualifications for leadership did you feel *least* qualified? *Most* qualified?

7. How long has it been since a discussion in your small group went *way* off course? What can you do to prevent that from happening again?

8. Is this group being led with a spirit of grace?

RECOMMENDED READING

A Passion for Faithfulness: Wisdom from the Book of Nehemiah by J.I. Packer (Wheaton, IL: Crossway Books, 1995)

Recovering Biblical Manhood and Womanhood, edited by John Piper and Wayne Grudem (Wheaton, IL: Crossway Books, 1991)

The Making of a Leader by J. Robert Clinton (Colorado Springs, CO: NavPress, 1988)

Spiritual Leadership by J. Oswald Sanders (Chicago, IL: Moody Press, 1994)

CHAPTER FIVE

THE ART OF CARE AND CORRECTION

MICKEY CONNOLLY

As we read in Chapter One of this book, a primary goal of small-group ministry is sanctification. God has called us each to be conformed to the image of Christ. In God's wisdom, he has made us so that we cannot accomplish this without the involvement of others. Wayne Grudem has said, "Sanctification is usually a corporate process in the New Testament. It is something that happens in community."[1] Another has well said, "One can acquire anything in solitude except character."

The primary roadblock to both personal maturity and biblical relationships is sin: sin in our own life; sin in others' lives; a world fallen because of sin. In each of these areas we can find great help and hope in the committed relationships that can grow out of small groups. To assist us in our ongoing quest to become more like Christ, God uses people in three ways—to reveal our sin, to help us to take action against our sin, and to walk with us in our struggle against sin.

First, God uses people to help reveal our sin. As friends observe our life "up close and personal," they can point out areas of sin and weakness and/or simply areas where we might need to grow. Also, interaction with others *reveals* our sins as situations reveal what is in our hearts.

Once sin is exposed, God gives us others who help us deal with our sin through confrontation, counseling, encouragement, accountability, and prayer. Finally, he gives us others to help and support us as we face the effects of living in a sinful world—pain, discouragement, confusion, weakness—while we "wait to be liberated from the bondage of decay and brought into the glorious freedom of the children of God" (Ro 8:21).

Let's take a look at this last aspect first.

> ❝ The Christian approach is to solve all problems, not just solve some problems or solve them part way. Romans 5:20 tells us about the fullness of God's grace: 'But where sin abounded, grace far more abounded.' That assurance means that when Christ meets sin, He more than meets the need. It is not His concern to 'patch things up' or even to turn back the clock. He wants to turn a bad thing into a great one! And He will settle for nothing less.[2] ❞
>
> — Jay Adams

Caring for One Another

There are many ways we can express care for others in our small group. Let me suggest five proven methods.

Comfort. To comfort means to cheer or to ease the grief and troubles of life. Life can be hard. We can face serious trials and tragedy—the death of a family member or close friend, loss of a job, a broken relationship we struggle to reconcile. We also face daily disappointments and hardships that can trouble and burden us. Sometimes we just have a bad day. How wonderful it is at times like these to have committed friends who will gather around us, bring comfort, and help ease our burdens.

Meditate on 2 Corinthians 1:3-4. When God comforts us in our troubles, what does he expect us to do in turn?

The New Testament instructs us to "mourn with those who mourn" (Ro 12:15) and to "comfort those in any trouble with the comfort we ourselves have received from God" (2Co 1:4). I regularly meet with a group of men in our church for accountability and support. I can think of many times over the years when we have helped each other through trials at work or at home, through difficult and discouraging struggles with sin, or simply through life's ups and downs. The comfort received and given in these times has been an invaluable help in our walk with God through a fallen world.

Counsel. By this I don't mean formal counseling, but sharing with those in need the wisdom, insight, and experience we have gained. Paul told the Romans, "I myself am convinced, my brothers, that you yourselves are full of goodness, complete in knowledge and competent to instruct one another" (Ro 15:14). My wife and her friends excel at this. In an hour of chatting on the phone they can solve all the problems of the world (at least their worlds) in an informal yet extremely biblical, practical, and effective way. They provide a listening ear. They share what God has been teaching them, or what has worked for them in practical and spiritual matters.

Warning to men: Don't try this! You are not genetically constituted to just chat for an hour. For men, something resembling chatting is only beneficial when done in the context of an activity such as fishing, eating, or watching football. Here is an actual transcript (well, more or less) of a close male-bonding experience:

Gettin' any bites?
Yep.
(Pause) What bait you usin'?
Uh…minnows.
(Long pause) Do you think I should become a missionary in Tibet?
Nope.
(Medium pause) Think I should switch to artificial lures?
(Reflective pause) Well…Firetigers always work for me this time of year.
Huh.
Yeah…they're good.
Huh.

Among other things, this conversation demonstrates the natural male tendency to focus more on peripheral issues (such as fishing lures) than on far more significant personal matters (such as a possible call to evangelism). So heads up, guys—you probably need to pay especially close attention to this chapter.

Encourage. To encourage means to inspire with courage, spirit, and hope; to hearten; to urge forward. Everyone occasionally gets discouraged. We face times when life seems difficult, progress slow, or challenges insurmountable. How important it is at these times to have someone give us a pep-talk based not on positive thinking or blind optimism but on the manifold promises and hope held out to us in the Scriptures.

At other times, when we let our priorities get out of line, our zest for pressing ahead begins to slip away. We give in to the temptation to settle down and take it easy, and our pursuit of God shifts into neutral. At such times, we need someone to come alongside and exhort us onward. I believe this is what the writer of Hebrews refers to when he says, "Let us consider how we may spur one another on toward love and good deeds" (Heb 10:24).

Lastly, encouragement can come from expressions of appreciation and thanks. "You've done a good job," "I've noticed the way you have persevered in faith and joy through your trial," "Thanks for the way you served," and similar expressions of affirmation are all deeply encouraging to hear. I can't tell you how often I have been buoyed

For Further Study:
Job got high marks from his friends for his ability to encourage (see Job 4:3-4). How would you rate his wife's gift in this area? (See Job 2:7-10)

63

in spirit and freshly motivated to mature and serve through this kind of encouragement from others.

Help. All of the above are important expressions of care for one another, but not the only expressions. There are many ways we can also physically and materially help those in our small group. James reminds us, "If one of you says…'Go, I wish you well; keep warm and well fed,' but does nothing about his physical needs, what good is it?" (Jas 2:16). He said this not to discount the importance of our words but to point out that in many situations words alone can't meet the need. Meals for families with a new-born, helping someone put a new roof on his house, providing financial help to someone temporarily out of work, giving someone a ride to a meeting—in all these and many more practical ways we are to serve those in our small group.

My family and I are preparing to move, and a week before my house was to go on the market I still had several major fix-up projects to complete. I would never have been able to get everything done in time myself, but a dozen friends gave up a Saturday to come help me. In no time at all, the jobs were done. This was not only a huge practical blessing to me and my family, but a great time of building my friendships with these men.

1 Of the gifts listed in Romans 12:6-8, which ones would apply most directly to helping one another in obvious, practical ways?

Correct. Most people don't think of correcting or being corrected as part of our care for one another, but in fact it is one of the most vital ways we serve our friends. Remember, sin is the primary enemy of both personal maturity and our relationships with others. To correct means literally "to straighten up again"; to intervene and help when someone is going off course. What could be more valuable to a friend than this? The Scriptures counsel us to love correction, going so far as to say that those who hate correction are stupid (Pr 12:1).

Let's spend the rest of this chapter looking at this vital area of ministry to one another. As we do so, let our heart attitude be one of trying to see how we can be more effective in helping one another both to grow personally and to work through the difficulties our sin causes in our relationships. The main skills of correction can be summarized as conflict resolution, confrontation, and confession.

For Further Study:
Read Hebrews 12:5-8. How does God treat those he loves? Do you think it would be kind for you to treat your friends the same way?

64

Resolving Conflicts

Conflict and offense are inevitable. When we mix with people who are sinful and selfish (that is, people who are just like us), we expose ourselves to the possibility of conflict and offense. Where might this happen? How about any place on earth! But it's especially likely where we are relating closely to others—at home, at church, in school, at work, in our neighborhood...or in our small group.

Disagreement is inevitable because people are different from one another. Conflict and offense are likely (in any given circumstance) because we are sinful. But disagreement need not always lead to conflict, nor conflict to offense. You can disagree with someone without sinning and you can be sinned against without taking offense. Sometimes, you might *perceive* an offense even when no one has sinned against you—in which case the only thing that was "offended" was your own pride, self-centeredness, or some other idol in your heart. There are also other possibilities, some of them discussed later in this chapter. Discernment, honest inquiry, and wise application of the Scriptures are critical.

> ❝ The Bible teaches that we should see conflict neither as an inconvenience nor as an occasion for selfish gain, but rather as an opportunity to demonstrate the presence and power of God....it encourages us to look at conflict as an opportunity to glorify God, to serve others, and to grow to be like Christ.[3] ❞
>
> — **Ken Sande**

This much is certain. While our goal is to love one another genuinely and fully, we *will* have disagreements. And we *will* have conflicts during which we sin against others and are sinned against. Jesus himself said, "Temptations to sin are sure to come" (Lk 17:1, RSV). However, just because they are sure to come doesn't mean that, when they do come, we aren't responsible for resolving them in a godly and redemptive manner.

In fact, trying to avoid the godly resolution of conflicts just builds a dam between ourselves and others, allowing a reservoir of misunderstanding, bitterness, unforgiveness, and/or resentment to form. The dam eventually bursts, producing problems far more serious than any we would have faced by dealing with our differences or concerns in the first place. In the meantime, as we keep shoring up the walls of the dam in a futile attempt to prevent them from bursting, our character becomes increasingly defined by our sinful attitudes. But none of these things need to

Meditate on 1 Peter 4:8. Here's a great strategy for avoiding needless conflicts.

Meditate on Proverbs 1:7. Whether we are correcting, being corrected, or just trying to determine whether correction is appropriate, what is the most important heart attitude we can have?

happen if we will diligently employ God's methods for avoiding and resolving conflict.

Avoiding conflict. I once heard it said, "It is better to build a guard rail at the top of a cliff than to run an ambulance service at the bottom." This is especially true when it comes to our relationships. Our first goal is to be aware of potential pitfalls so we can head off conflicts at the pass.

There are several dangerous but common ways of seeking to avoid conflict. Trying not to talk about potentially volatile subjects or areas of disagreement is a typical but unsuitable strategy. Hoping a problem area will disappear doesn't work either. Neither does switching small groups every six months or living in a cave. These all represent efforts to ignore the fact that we're on a road with lots of cliffs, pretty heavy traffic, some inconsiderate drivers, and no guard rails. But in truth, because the hazards are so prevalent, these attempts do not avoid *conflict* so much as they avoid its resolution!

The far better way is to take steps to prevent conflicts from happening in the first place—to build those spiritual guard rails. We do this by practicing the kind of regular and honest communication that keeps us current with our friends, enables us to know them, and lets them know us. These efforts build a quality of relationship that helps us handle differences more easily when they arise. As part of our communication, we should also be inviting input and evaluation from our friends on a regular basis. This gives them a convenient context in which to share concerns about us or our relationship.

Having realistic (not low) expectations will also help. No one in your group is perfect, including you. Taking into account our friends' maturity, circumstances, limitations, and humanity will help us extend grace to one another. God "remembers that we are dust" (Ps 103:14). We ought graciously to remember the same about one another. The more clearly we can communicate our expectations to each other, the less likely we will be to find offense.

Finally, we must deal with little things. We don't have to deal with

2 Which of the following methods, commonly in use in homes, schools, and workplaces around the world, resolve conflicts as effectively as the biblical approach?

❑ Spending the rest of your life ignoring everyone with whom you've had a conflict.

❑ Being extra nice to the offended party the next time you happen to see him or her.

❑ If an attempt at reconciliation is made, insisting no offense was taken (even if it was).

❑ Getting as many people as possible to think badly of the person with whom you had the conflict.

❑ Acting like it never happened (see "Being extra nice," above), firm in the belief that if the phrase "time heals all wounds" is not actually in the Bible, it ought to be.

everything; but if some little thing is bothering you, deal with it before it becomes a big thing.

Working through conflict. Conflicts may involve mere differences or genuine offense, and understanding the distinction is critical. Whichever it is, the following process will help you begin to find resolution. As you go through this process, keep in mind that your three-fold goal is to solve the problem, grow closer *in* the process, and become more godly *through* the process. Personal victory is *not* the goal, for this will neither bless your friend nor please God.

First, evaluate the conflict. Does it involve sin, or a mere disagreement over some personal preference? Here, there is no better wisdom regarding the *attitude* we are to have than James 1:19: "My dear brothers, take note of this: Everyone should be quick to listen, slow to speak and slow to become angry." Listening is the first, second, and third step we should take. This includes getting a grasp on the issues from both a material perspective (what happened) and a heart perspective (how it made each of you feel). It also involves trying to get a better understanding of the other person, to gain sympathy and compassion for him or her.

> ❝ To listen properly, a servant's attitude and posture is necessary. It requires us to put our whole inner and outer man at another person's disposal, saying: 'Your interests, concerns, problems, successes, or failures are more important than mine. I will listen to whatever you have to say as long as it is biblically proper. I will allow you to express yourself fully. I yield myself to you. Let's focus on what is most important to you rather than on what is most important to me.'[4] ❞
> — **Wayne Mack**

Next, stay on the subject. Cover only one issue at a time. Review what happened, *not* your assessment of the other person's motives and character (such assessments are often sinful and inaccurate). Also, do not—in an effort to "win points"—bring up incidents from the past that you have already forgiven.

When the time does come to speak, speak only that which will lead to understanding and resolution. Bring an attitude of respectful inquiry. Don't accuse, vent anger, or give voice to your self-pity (which is sin). Paul's counsel is sound: "Do not let any unwholesome talk come out of your mouths, but only what is helpful for building others up according to their needs, that it may benefit those who listen" (Eph 4:29). Here, dealing with your own faults first and foremost will help greatly.

For Further Study:
Have you ever said something that you immediately regretted? Before you invest in a muzzle, try memorizing Proverbs 10:19.

Confronting Sin in Others

Whether we have been sinned against on a given occasion, or become aware that a fellow believer has a pattern of sin in his life, confrontation may be in order. To confront is "to bring face to face." Here, confrontation is the process of getting face to face with someone to help him see a particular sin in his life or to work through conflict and offense and bring forgiveness and reconciliation. There is a right and a wrong way to do this.

In the case of a personal offense, the wrong way might go something like this. In the middle of your small-group meeting Joe interrupts while you are speaking. You go ballistic! "I'm sick and tired of you interrupting me all the time. You are the most insensitive, inconsiderate jerk I have ever met! You are so proud that you think what you have to say is more important than what anyone else is saying. I've been teasing you about this for months but you have never gotten the hint, so now let me tell you right to your face in front of everybody. You owe me an apology and I demand it right now!...I'm waiting!" This approach probably won't be fruitful.

What is the right way? The Scriptures lay out several principles to follow when confronting someone about sin.

First, determine if it is necessary to confront. You will need different standards for different situations.

Proverbs 19:11 says, "A man's wisdom gives him patience; it is to his glory to overlook an offense." It is not necessary to go to someone every time you are offended. If you are able, you can forgive and go on with a person without any negative effect on the relationship. But you may not simply chicken out. The incident must be resolved in your heart and mind. (If you have an open conflict it *must* be addressed—you can't just let these pass without resolution and reconciliation.)

In the final analysis, you must confront if you find that 1) you are unable to get the incident out of your mind, 2) you are unable to have a normal relationship with the person who has offended or sinned against you, or 3) you believe someone has something against you but is not coming to you—you don't have to know what it is, just that the person seems to be acting differently toward you.

For Further Study:
Read James 5:19-20. As you can see, the benefits of correcting a friend far outweigh the tension it may cause at first.

> **❝** Confrontation can be very difficult, and many avoid it. But what wasted time could be redeemed in our lives if faithful friends started telling us some truths about ourselves.[5] **❞**
>
> — **Terry Virgo**

68

When a friend is sinning and you believe you need to speak to him, you should ask yourself: Is this sin a pattern? Is it so serious that it needs immediate attention? Is this God's timing for me to confront? Am I the one to confront in this case? (These last two are not loophole questions for avoiding what you know you need to do.)

In general, you ought to confront when you believe the sin is ongoing and serious and when, in prayer, you do not sense that your attitudes and motives are wrong. Always remember that God is working on things in the other person's life as well. When you are called to confront you are called to come alongside the work the Holy Spirit is already doing in his life—not to *be* the Holy Spirit.

Second, define the problem. What are you confronting him about? What did he do or say? What sin is involved? What is the impact? How does he need to change? Defining the problem will help you be clear and concise when you go to confront him. Make sure you define things biblically, for it is Scripture alone—not our own thoughts and feelings—that is "God-breathed and is useful for teaching, rebuking, correcting and training in righteousness, so that the man of God may be thoroughly equipped for every good work" (2Ti 3:16-17).

> 66 Terms not only describe; they interpret. When we use a word such as gossip, many biblical images and exhortations come to mind—as well they should. When we try to describe the same activity in a more 'neutral' fashion, what we really do is describe it in an unbiblical way. God's descriptive categories are not neutral.... 'Neutrality' is really a surrender to unbelief. It is a refusal to speak and think from God's perspective.[6] 99
>
> — **E. Bradley Beevers**

Third, get the log out of your own eye. If you are confronting someone who has sinned against you, you will often find your own sin has contributed. If you are confronting another about a particular sin, Scripture warns you to be aware of your own sins and temptations in this same area (see Galatians 6:1). This isn't to say you ought not to confront, only that you are not to confront until you first examine your own heart and clear your own conscience. This will enable you to confront in humility and the fear of the Lord, increasing your effectiveness in bringing reconciliation, repentance, and resolution.

For Further Study: To see what Jesus said about removing logs from our eyes, turn to Matthew 7:1-5.

Self-examination can also help in another way. You might have become offended without there having been an offense—rather, someone may merely have done something to expose your selfishness or pride (you may think you are just "overly sensitive"). Likewise, you have to take care not to confront people about what you think is sin just because you don't appreciate some aspect of their personality. In such cases, you can start out confronting someone and end up in confession and repentance.

Fourth, prepare your heart. This involves three things. Make sure your *motives* are right—to glorify God, turn your brother or sister from sin, and be reconciled. (In other words, not to win your case, straighten them out, put them in their place, or relieve your irritation.) Make sure your *attitudes* are right—gentleness, patience, humility, and genuine concern for the welfare of others. Finally, *pray*— for effectiveness in communicating your concerns; for the person's heart to be prepared to receive; and for God's grace for repentance, forgiveness, and reconciliation.

Fifth, confront. Ultimately, God's grace will determine the effectiveness of any confrontation. However, there are several things you can do to make times of confrontation more effective.

Meditate on 1 Thessalonians 2:11-12. Paul spoke some pretty strong words to the churches...but what was the attitude of his heart?

3 Proverbs 18:13 and 18:17 help explain why it is that, when we think a brother or sister has sinned against us, we need to approach him or her with a humble and teachable heart. Read these passages, then write a sentence in the space below that expresses the essence of what these two verses say about us.

Speak to the person privately.

Plan for an atmosphere where distractions will be minimal so you can fully concentrate on the issues at hand.

Affirm your genuine affection for the person before you begin confronting. This isn't to somehow soften him up for the kill but to set a proper tone for your meeting. You *are* there to speak the truth...but in love (Eph 4:15). Many times I have seen the entire atmosphere of a meeting change when I began to communicate my love for the person even while confronting his sin.

Share your perceptions as honestly and clearly as possible. Use biblical language when explaining behaviors or sins (for example, say "pride" instead of "self-esteem"). Don't try to build an airtight case with mountains of evidence—you aren't a prosecutor seeking a conviction.

Maintain a spirit of inquiry. Don't assume your observations and conclusions are infallible and you know all the facts and motives involved. Recently, I had to confront a friend based on some concerns about his behavior. I communicated my concerns and asked for his perspective. Getting "the rest of the story" revealed the concerns were unfounded. He then told me how, the night before, someone had confronted him about the same issues but

STEPPING OUTSIDE
A Testimony

Through a mutual friend, I discovered that Tony, a member of my small group, had a habit of going to a neighborhood bar every payday to have drinks with his buddies from work. Before he was saved, Tony took hard drugs and drank excessively. He'd walked away from the drugs, but I was concerned that he not become trapped by this lingering habit of "having a drink with the guys."

Tony's a weight-lifter, a pretty intimidating guy. I felt I had to talk to him that afternoon. I wasn't sure how he'd react.

I found Tony at the bar with one of his friends. I greeted them both and then asked Tony if I could talk to him outside for a minute. He said, "Sure," in a surprised way.

Standing on the sidewalk, I told him that I was coming to him as his small-group leader and biblical friend. I explained how a Christian friend had to confront me about my drug habit even after I became a Christian. It changed my life. I let him know I cared about him enough to do the same thing.

He took it pretty well. He admitted it was embarrassing to have me stop by, but that he felt the conviction of the Holy Spirit. He went back inside, and I left feeling I had done what God wanted me to do, trusting him for the results in Tony's life.

That incident was a turning point for both of us. Now Tony is an integral part of a weekly men's group devoted to "confessing our sins and praying for one another that we may be healed." He doesn't shrink back from confronting me or anyone in the group. I've heard him say that this memorable incident helped him see the critical need for confrontation to battle sin and resolve conflicts in our lives! I've also gained confidence to lead the group and challenge people if I see stumbling blocks to spiritual growth.

— Glenn Umek (Garfield Heights, OH)

with guns blazing, accusations flying, and assumptions ruling. My friend obviously appreciated the difference. Your friends will appreciate it, too.

Offer biblical counsel and solutions. Be prepared to present an appropriate course of action. Try to help the person formulate a plan to resist temptation or be accountable. If you don't feel capable of doing this yourself, refer him to your small-group leader or a pastor in your church.

Provide sufficient time, if necessary, for him to think through what you have presented—don't demand an immediate response.

Pray with and for the person.

Finally, *follow up*. Too often we confront but fail to make sure our confrontation was effective and the results lasting. If things went well, follow up within a couple of days to express affection and appreciation for your friend's response and to find out how things have been going in the process of change. This is also a good time to see if he has any questions or further thoughts on the things you shared. He may even request that you serve him by holding him accountable as he seeks to change.

If things did not go well or if he asked for some time to consider what you said, follow up to see what

Meditate on Psalm 141:5. What was David's attitude toward the prospect of being corrected by another believer? Is this how you feel?

progress has been made. He may choose not to respond to your correction. If that happens, don't give up. Proceed to the next level of confrontation Jesus laid out for us: "But if he will not listen, take one or two others along, so that 'every matter may be established by the testimony of two or three witnesses'" (Mt 18:16). While other passages discussed in this chapter specify the crucial heart attitudes we are to take into each such confrontation, Matthew 18:15-17 provides the practical steps we must follow when facing a difficult confrontation.

Responding to confrontation. Just as there is a biblical way to confront, there is also a biblical way to respond to confrontation. If someone confronts you about a sin or offense, you can help in several ways to ensure the process has a genuinely redemptive outcome. First, listen humbly and prayerfully. Second, confess and ask forgiveness where possible. If you need some time to process and pray about what has been said, ask for it. (But if you tend to do this every time you are corrected, please hear me: you need to check your heart carefully for pride and unteachableness.) Just make sure you get back to the person. Last, thank and affirm the person for coming. He or she has just served you significantly by pointing out a sin or seeking to reconcile your relationship.

4 Galatians 6:2 reads: "Carry each other's burdens, and in this way you will fulfill the law of Christ." List three or four ways discussed in this chapter by which we can "carry each other's burdens."

1)

2)

3)

4)

Now, put a star by any that you have practiced in the past two weeks.

Confessing Our Own Sins

I've spent a lot of time discussing what to do when other people sin. However, it is far more important to regularly examine our hearts to identify instances where *we* may have sinned. We should not have to wait to confess until someone has confronted us with our sins or a breach in our relationship. When we realize we have sinned against someone or offended him, *or even think we have,* we should go to him and make things right. Again, there is a right and a wrong way to do this.

"Well I guess maybe I might have sinned against you a little but only because you did such-and-such first, so I guess maybe I owe you an apology if you were offended." This does not meet the biblical criteria. Then what does?

For starters, thoroughly examine your conscience.

Determine, with the help of the Holy Spirit, where you have sinned. Ask for conviction and godly sorrow for each of those sins.

For Further Study:
What's the difference between godly sorrow and worldly sorrow? (See 2 Corinthians 7:9-11)

When you get together with the one you have sinned against (and don't wait for these meetings to "just happen"—*make* them happen), confess your sins honestly, clearly, specifically, and completely. This means you confess not only your words and actions but your motives as well. *Never gloss over your sins, offer excuses for your behavior, or generalize.* ("Sometimes I can tend to be harsh" is pale and ineffective compared to "I was harsh to you when I said such-and-such.") This will not be difficult if you have godly sorrow for your sin. Ken Sande's insight is helpful here: "Specific admissions help to convince others that you are honestly facing up to what you have done, which makes it easier for them to forgive you."[7] Remember, the goal is not just to clear your conscience but to gain reconciliation with the one you have sinned against.

Express sorrow for what you have done and for the consequences of your actions. By this you are letting the person know that you realize your actions have affected him or her by causing pain, anxiety, or difficulty. It also lets the person know you are willing to accept any consequences that may accompany your confession (such as repayment of damages, going to others who may have been drawn in by gossip, etc.). Also, identify the lessons you have learned from the experience and specific ways you are going to change as a result. This will give the person hope and trust for the future and will help him or her to see how seriously you are taking your sin.

For Further Study:
Read James 3:18. What (in addition to peace) results from our efforts to be "peacemakers"?

Finally, ask for forgiveness. To actually say the words, "Would you forgive me?" is important—for forgiveness is indeed what we need and are seeking.

5 Imagine that you need to confess a serious sin to someone and ask his or her forgiveness. Rank the following approaches in order of which is best.

❏ Make a telephone call

❏ Have a personal meeting

❏ Send an E-mail

❏ Ask your spouse or a friend to take care of it for you

Responding to a confession. A godly response to a confession includes several elements. First, tell the person you forgive him or her. *Do not say "It's OK" or "Don't worry about it."* (Sins are never OK or not to be worried about. Rather, they are to be forgiven.) Second, thank the one seeking forgiveness for coming and confessing. Affirm your love and respect for the person. It takes courage and humility to confess sins—to do so is to serve another and to help build a godly relationship. Third, ask if he or she has any offense toward you as a result of the incident, or —if applicable—confess any sin you may have contributed to the incident. Lastly, declare the episode over—dead and gone—and express your intent to walk fully reconciled to the person.

This Stuff Works!

Let me finish with a personal testimony to the value of correction. My wife Jane and I meet annually with some other couples to evaluate our marriages. One year, our evaluation was going well and I was feeling smug and safe. (In fact, as I often do, I started thinking ahead to lunch—but we will save discussion of that sin for another day!) Suddenly I heard Jane speak these dreaded words: "Well, there is one thing I would like to bring up." I knew I was about to experience…The Joy of Correction!

Jane told how at times I quickly dismiss her desires and opinions, expressing my own opinions in a strong and authoritative way. (Here's the translation: I was proud and selfish.) She gave several excellent examples. One of the other wives piped up, "Oh yeah, I remember when you did that." (Did she really have to include a dead-ringer imitation of my arrogantly dismissive hand gesture?) One of the guys said I've treated him the same way. By the time we were finished, they had helped me explore the roots of my sins, see the impact of my sins on others, and gain insight on how to change. We ended with confession, forgiveness, and prayer. The whole discussion took only about a half hour, but it was life-changing.

I thank God for a good wife and good friends who are willing to correct and able to do it effectively. This

> " Through forgiveness God tears down the walls that our sins have erected, and he opens the way for a renewed relationship with him. This is exactly what we must do if we are to forgive as the Lord forgives us; we must release the person who has wronged us from the penalty of being separated from us. Because we must not hold wrongs against others, not think about them, and not punish others for them, forgiveness may be described as a decision to make four promises:
> 'I will no longer dwell on this incident.'
> 'I will not bring up this incident again and use it against you.'
> 'I will not talk to others about this incident.'
> 'I will not allow this incident to stand between us or hinder our relationship.'
> By making and keeping these promises, you tear down the walls that stand between you and your offender. You promise not to punish by holding the person at a distance. You clear the way for your relationship to develop unhindered by memories of past wrongs. This is exactly what God does for us, and it is what he commands us to do for others.[8] "
>
> — Ken Sande

was true biblical care that helped me, blessed others, and pleased God. Our Father intends each of his children to live in the special blessings that flow from the application of biblical correction. Take this material to heart. Put it to work in your small group. God guarantees that it works. ■

GROUP DISCUSSION

1. This is a fun one: According to most translations of the Bible, Christ told Peter to forgive someone, not seven times, but seventy times seven—or 490 times (Mt 18:22). However, no one has ever found the verse indicating the specific vengeance you can take on those who commit their 491st offense against you. What would the ideal vengeance be? Here are a few ideas to get things rolling:

- Wire their home, car, and workplace for sound and require that they listen to the 24-hour polka station non-stop for six months.
- Make them listen repeatedly to every Academy Awards acceptance speech given since the inception of the ceremony in 1928.
- Make them speak politely and at length with every telephone salesman who calls their home during the next year. In each of these conversations, they must say at least once: "I'm so glad you called," "Why, of course!", and "Oh, absolutely."

2. Do we benefit more from giving care or receiving care in the church?

3. Can you describe an experience in which you had a disagreement that did not grow into a conflict—or one that did when it should not have?

4. What's the difference between saying "I'm sorry" and "Please forgive me"?

5. In what ways have you personally benefited from giving or receiving biblical correction?

6. Try role-playing two types of confrontation: one which starts with an accusation and another which starts with an inquiry. Why does tone make such a difference?

7. The author says "open conflicts" must be addressed (see page 68). How do you know when one has taken place?

8. Can you think of five *un*biblical phrases people might use to shift attention away from their sin? (Example: "Yeah, I know I should have called you sooner, but I was really bummed out.")

RECOMMENDED READING *The Peacemaker* by Ken Sande (Grand Rapids, MI: Baker Book House, 1991)

CHAPTER SIX

NEVER SAY COMFORTABLE

JOHN BUTLER

No doubt you've heard the expressions many times: "Find your comfort level"…"What are you comfortable with?"… "As comfortable as an old pair of shoes."

We love our comfort, don't we? Our urge to pursue pleasure is deep and universal. Yet there are many places in our lives where God desires to put this urge to death. This may sound harsh, but I know from personal experience—including many confrontations over my own love of comfort—that it is true. Small groups can provide excellent opportunities for us to die to excessive love of comfort by embracing the changes and challenges God brings our way.

One day many years ago, our pastor announced a change in the small-group strategy. For a year we had been leading our small-group members into closer relationships. It had been a lot of work, but we had made real progress, and several new believers were attending. Exciting things were taking place in these new Christians' lives. Now, due to a new approach to small groups, there would be some reorganization. As leaders, we might have some of the same folks in our "new" groups, but things were definitely going to change.

We had an expression back then (used when someone was about to get yanked through a keyhole): "Constant change is here to stay." I hated that expression. And I did not like the new strategy my pastor was adopting.

What was I experiencing? The challenge of change, made worse by selfishness and a prideful attitude. In my view, we had worked hard to get our group to a healthy place, and now had to let it go. The lesson here is how easily small-group leaders (and members) can become self-absorbed and territorial. We can forget that small groups are intended to serve the goals of the local church—that they are not ends in themselves. There are higher purposes than just "our group."

The approach to small groups in our church has matured over the years. Some of these changes have posed challenges to our comfort levels. Even simple things such as a renewed emphasis on evangelism, the addition of new people, changes in leadership, or some other shift in member-ship can seem unwelcome. Without keeping the mis-sion of the local church in view, small groups become isolated and ingrown.

Make Way for New People!

For Further Study:
Read Proverbs 25:16. Does the Bible tell us we can have "too much of a good thing"?

Small groups are often very effective in providing members with care and true fellowship. It is not uncom-mon to see close bonds of friendship form within groups, especially if the groups are pursuing biblical fellowship. Could there be anything wrong with something as good and as scriptural as this? Can there be too much of a good thing? Sometimes, yes. Even biblical fellowship, when pursued with the wrong motives, can tempt us to adopt false priorities.

My neighbor recently found termites all over his living room rug, and swarms of them in his yard (the yard *right next* to mine!). I'm hoping pest-control efforts have per-manently solved the problem. But as scary a sight as swarms of termites may be, these vermin are far more dangerous when they remain unseen. A home infested with termites can look perfectly normal on the outside, yet all the while the structure is being weakened.

Something similar can happen with small groups. Just as homeowners must stay on the lookout for termites, small-group members must be on guard against *koinonitis*, that deadly foe of healthy groups and healthy churches. This strange word is a humorous extension of the term *koinonia*, the New Testament Greek word for biblical fellowship.

"Koinonitis" is a kind of "disease" we catch when we start loving *koinonia* too much—for example, to the

1 You arrive for your small-group meeting and see 1) a table set with plates of brownies, 2) some visitors sitting together in a corner, and 3) your best friend waving from across the room. Which place will you go first?

exclusion of evangelism—and thus become ingrown and selfish. This sinful tendency must be resisted wholeheartedly. There must always be room in our hearts to embrace those whom God is adding to us, without any sense of intrusion or inconvenience. Indeed, small groups are excellently suited to evangelizing the lost and discipling new believers.

In the small group. In our church (for the reasons set forth in Chapter One), we ask that our members be involved in a small group. This expectation is communicated in our literature, our messages, our church membership course, and elsewhere. Therefore, we try to make it easy for new people to become involved in this aspect of church life. Yet there are some natural obstacles.

Imagine you are going to a small-group meeting for the first time and you don't know anyone, or maybe just one or two people. Most people find it intimidating to walk into a house full of strangers. Guests don't always know what to anticipate or what is expected of them. I know of a man who thought the dress code was fairly formal for small-group meetings, so he wore his Sunday best. He felt awkward as the members of the group arrived very casually dressed.

A group that has met for any length of time develops its own culture (some very bizarre, I might add)—a "local dialect," certain food rituals, inside jokes, even possibly its own time zone (for example, a starting time of 7:00 p.m. Eastern Standard Time may be the equivalent of 7:20 p.m. Eastern Small Group Time)! It's easy for first-timers to feel uncomfortable.

In addition, our lives become busy. We develop patterns of socializing that may leave little room for newcomers to the small group—a regular "family time," sports activities, children's play time, coffee together. These are good and valuable, but we must guard against any appearance of becoming "cliquish" or exclusive in our behavior and attitudes. These things are sin and have no place in our small groups.

Consequently, all of us must reject the selfish tendency to gravitate only toward those in our group whom we know best...to sit by the same people and talk about our common interests—sports, hobbies, our children, whatever. Over time it's easy to settle into comfortable relationships, even feeling some annoyance at newcomers or, for that matter, anyone in the group who might dare to break our routine. In fact, sometimes believers can treat newcomers to the church as if they are somehow unworthy of our attention. The root of this tendency is self-centeredness—yet Scripture charges us to think of others as more important than ourselves (Php 2:3).

Meditate on Romans 12:10. How could you apply this verse in relating to a visitor in your group?

A church is not to be a closed culture, but a place of life and hope for the desperate. As the church, we are called to disciple the nations, welcoming all who will enter. What do you do—personally—to ensure guests feel welcome at your meetings? Are guests simply the leader's responsibility or do you take it upon yourself, whatever your role in the group, to get involved? (Any signs of koinonitis?) Here are some suggestions.

- Greet guests and invite them to be a part of your conversation by introducing them to others in the group. "Ed, have you met Mike yet? This is his first time here."

Meditate on Romans 12:13. What is the main thing you share when you practice hospitality? Yourself!

- Consider how to involve guests in your activities during the week. "Hey Mike—a bunch of the guys are going to watch the game tomorrow night at my house. Can you come over and hang out with us?"
- Take an interest in their lives and care for them. Find out about their world and if there are ways to serve them through prayer, practical help, or encouragement.

Next, ask yourself these questions about your friendships:

- How long has it been since I included someone new in my regular activities?
- Do others feel welcome to become involved in my conversations and activities?
- What steps have I taken to include someone new in what I'm doing?
- Am I willing to widen my circle of relationships?
- If not, why?

Paul appeals to us to "look not only to your own interests, but also to the interests of others" (Php 2:4). Are we willing to share our friends and ourselves with new people? (Any signs of koinonitis yet?)

At the Sunday meeting. When people visit a church for the first time, they may face hurdles no less difficult than those of first-time visitors to a small group. Will the pastor and message be orthodox, understandable, and relatable?

What style of worship music is played there? What ministries are available for children and teens?

For better or worse, churches answer one critical question for guests almost immediately: "Will there be room for me here?" Consider the following issues.

- What kind of welcome will visitors receive when they are identified?
- Will someone go out of his way to greet them warmly?
- Will someone help them find their way around the building?
- Will anyone build a relational bridge through an invitation to lunch or a follow-up visit or telephone call?

Please don't answer these questions hastily. Ask them again—and ask them *of yourself*, not just of your church. How are you really doing in these areas? When was the last time *you* took the initiative toward a guest?

The responsibility for welcoming new people falls on every church member. Through our attitudes and actions, we can "tell" people that our church simply has no room for them. When we do this, new people look elsewhere, or they may give up on church altogether. We must personally, actively, make room for new people. A large percentage of those who decide to stay in a church have been the recipients of someone's personal interest and initiative. Do you feel personal responsibility to welcome and include guests in the life of the church? (Look again, any signs of koinonitis *yet*?)

For Further Study:
Read 2 Corinthians 7:2. What was Paul's appeal to the church at Corinth? How much room is there in your heart for new people?

2 James 2:1-4 warns us against the sin of favoritism—in this case, treating well-dressed visitors to our meetings better than we treat poorly dressed ones. But favoritism can take many forms. Which of the following forms of favoritism have been a problem for you? (Check any that apply.)

When visitors are	Rather than
❏ Unattractive	Attractive
❏ Withdrawn	Outgoing
❏ Of another race	Of your race
❏ Apparently sad	Apparently happy
❏ About your age	Significantly older/younger
❏ Different in their lifestyle or dress	A lot like you in those areas

Many Hands Make Light Work

The small-group leader is limited in his capacity to care effectively for everyone. I recently spoke with a small-group leader's wife who said poignantly, "It's so exhausting to be the only one reaching out...."

Fortunately, in this case those words expressed a contrast with the past. A number of people from several small groups had gone out of their way to welcome a foreign student. The student returned to his home country challenged by the gospel and by the love he had felt from so many in our church. But my guess is that countless small-group leaders have uttered the same sort of statement—out of frustration: "It's so exhausting to be the only one...."

No heroes necessary. When you do help out, how do you perceive your own acts of service? When everyone pitches in with the right attitude, a group can make a tremendous impact. Make this your goal. Make it the status quo in your group.

I have a friend who was a U.S. Army Airborne Ranger infantry officer. Although he was already an infantry officer when he applied to Ranger School, at some point—like all Rangers—he made the decision that being a "regular" army guy was not enough...that the intense additional training needed to be a Ranger was worth the effort... that jumping out of an airplane would be fun...that being thrown into the most demanding and dangerous combat situations was not just a job, but an adventure!

Too often, I consider myself some kind of "Special Forces" soldier, a "breed apart" because of some puny act of service that challenged me in some small way! We can all be tempted to feel this way about serving others. But that's just pride—because serving people is normal New Testament Christianity, not some elite operation requiring heroic effort.

> **44** The duties of the Ministry will constantly exercise Christian self-denial. Thus it was with our Master. His food and rest were even foregone or forgotten in his absorbing delight in saving souls. Seasons of necessary retirement were interrupted without an upbraiding word. Hunger, thirst, cold, or fatigue set no bounds to the determined forgetfulness of Himself.[1] **77**
>
> **— Charles Bridges**

Personal growth through caring. As you get to know new people in your small group, you are likely to find yourself passing on to them some insight or wisdom regarding the Christian life. It just happens that way. But even on such informal occasions, difficult questions can arise that have no easy answers. And that's often OK—God stretches us at times. Needs of others in the small group teach us to put our love into action. Again, Paul tells us that we are "called to be free. But do not use your freedom to indulge the sinful nature; rather serve one another in love" (Gal 5:13).

Meditate on Luke 22:25-27. This passage directly challenges a core concept of worldly thinking. Does it challenge you, too?

Obviously, not everyone is able to handle all situations. But as the needs of new folks arise, our own heart attitudes are revealed. Will we accept inconvenience in order to serve?

People confronted with meeting a practical need or trying to share an insight on a difficult issue grow as a result of making themselves available. Do we belong to a small group because as a member we are served and blessed—or because we recognize God's call to serve others? When our focus is on the second reason, the first will take care of itself.

> **❝** Serving others usually requires no special talent or ability. But it does take a servant attitude to want to serve others, as well as an observant eye and mind to see what needs to be done. If we have a servant attitude, we can develop an observant eye. The reason most of us do not see opportunities to serve is that we are continually thinking about ourselves instead of others.[2] **❞**
>
> **— Jerry Bridges**

In fact, as responsibility for the care of newcomers is distributed throughout the group, members who come into a "caring" role can experience great personal growth as they are tested and challenged. Among other things, selfishness is revealed and, ideally, confronted. Comfort levels are stretched, and maturity levels rise. Serving others, in whatever capacity, makes us more like Christ!

Several years ago a family in our church was in a horrible auto accident. The husband, wife (seven months pregnant), and their two young sons were injured. The couple lost their baby and the wife suffered through a lengthy recovery from her injuries. Their small group, along with the church, responded unselfishly to meet practical needs, pray, and provide comfort. Not only did this couple receive effective care, but the wife's parents were deeply moved by the example of Christianity they saw. Their response was, "There really are caring and loving people in church."

For Further Study:
Read John 13:34-35. What is it about Christian love that makes it stand out so clearly to everyone?

Neighbors were amazed by the house-cleaning crews, provision of meals, and sheer number of friends showing up. In a dramatic demonstration of Christianity, a small group took practical, loving action and the members grew in Christ-likeness.

Starting New Groups

It's an unsettling experience. Maybe you've been there, too. One day some time ago I began pulling on my favorite pants, only to discover, to my dismay, that there was more *me* than there was pants. Without my ever noticing, the ol' body had subtly begun moving south. (Whenever I tell this story, certain friends question my use of the term "subtly." In their concern for accuracy, they also note that, technically speaking, this was not an *un*settling experience, but one involving a *settling* of my mid-section.)

The pants problem was one of capacity. Those particular pants were made for someone approximately the size I had once been! We see a similar dynamic at work in small groups—all have a certain capacity. When the natural capacity is exceeded, discomfort follows. The level of care and overall effectiveness of a small group can diminish greatly if the group grows too large. An oversized group often produces frustrated members who may drift away from involvement. Suddenly the group grows smaller again—but for the wrong reasons!

Small groups benefit by growing...and then multiplying before they get too large. If our small groups are effective at care, outreach, biblical fellowship, and the use of spiritual gifts, they will naturally attract people. (Who doesn't want to be part of a group that works?) The key to a healthy, growing group is the attitude of the individual member. Each must contribute to the growth of his or her group and do what is needed to help sustain the momentum of that growth.

For Further Study:
When a vibrant community of believers proclaims the gospel in bold, clear terms, what is the result? (See Acts 2:47 and 5:14)

If this is the attitude of the members, growth will be exciting because of the sense of *ownership* each one feels. Numerical growth within the group will be rewarding for everyone, not just one or two people. Active participation will position the group to multiply more easily because of the shared workload, common mission, and willingness to be used by the Lord in the service of his people.

The benefits to creating more small groups are numerous. New groups keep us in "adventure mode." New groups allow for the release of new leadership into the church. And new groups mean more room for those the Lord adds to the local church.

3 Which of the following traits suggests that members of a small group are in "adventure mode"?

❑ Members regularly ask God to show them new ways to serve in the group

❑ The group goes skydiving together once a month

❑ Koinonitis is less popular than room-temperature coffee

❑ Members have more good outreach ideas than they can possibly implement

❑ The official group snack food changes from cookies to sushi

Releasing New Leadership

My wife and I often tease our young daughter by telling her she can't celebrate any more birthdays. Our point is that, at her current age, she is the picture of perfect cuteness, so we want to keep her just as she is. Somehow, she is not particularly open to that idea. She wants to be a big girl. I guess I understand. I, too, would not have grown as a person or leader if someone had not given me room to mature.

Today, by God's grace, I am a pastor serving a church in the Virginia Beach area. But I didn't just wake up one day like Rip Van Winkle from his nap to discover I was in pastoral ministry. Over the years, there was a very real process of growth and adjustment as I chose to embrace new ministry opportunities.

In fact, I needed someone to push me along. It would not have been healthy for me to remain, in effect, a new believer for years. God desires us all to be increasingly fruitful in our service to him.

Shortly after we married, my wife and I were privileged to be involved in the early stages of a new church. The experience proved very beneficial to our growth. I began leading worship and carrying some responsibility for a small group. Soon I was asked to lead a small group. Eventually, through many stages, I came into full-time ministry. I know firsthand the benefits of being trained and released into new spheres of service, and I am grateful for the way God used wise friends to encourage me to accept new challenges. There's no question that many people are simply an invitation away from greater ministry responsibility in the local church.

During my years in pastoral ministry, I have approached numerous people about the prospect of leading a small group. The nearly universal response has been, "Me? Now? But I'm not ready!" Undaunted, I like to encourage them that God wants to help them grow and that, while I could be wrong, I believe I see in them some measure of leadership gifting.

Pastors should consider it a primary responsibility of their ministry to make ways for new leaders to emerge. A wise leader warns that pastors ought not "raise the bar of qualification ever higher" so that it becomes increasingly difficult for new leadership to emerge. A pastor should continually be on the lookout for those he can train, and for opportunities to release those who can lead effectively.

The pastors I am privileged to serve with are vitally interested in equipping and releasing people into the ministry giftings God distributes by his Spirit.

For Further Study:
Read Exodus 3:10-11; 4:1,10,13. How did God transform this apparently faithless, reluctant man into one of the most dynamic leaders in history?

4 To become the holder of the world record in the high jump, you must be able to clear a height of more than eight feet. What was the standard at the first modern Olympic Games in 1896?

To become the winning driver of the Indy 500, you must maintain an average speed of more than 160 mph. What was the standard at the first Indy 500 in 1911?

To become a small-group leader in a local church, you must meet the criteria set forth in Scripture. What was the standard in 200 A.D.?

(See answer key at page 86.)

"Instead of monopolizing ministry himself," writes John Stott of the pastor, "he actually multiplies ministries."[3] It is through this process of training and releasing that the church will be built and people brought to maturity.

A local church that does not train and release new leaders will be less effective. Small-group leaders are essential to the life of a church. There is simply no way a pastor or even a pastoral team can, by themselves, effectively care for all the people in a growing church. The Holy Spirit is faithful to distribute gifts of leadership, wisdom, mercy, discernment, etc., to individuals in the church to help provide care for *all* his people. It is a joy to watch spiritual gifts flourish as someone embraces the challenge of leading a small group. It is a joy to see the pastoral ministry multiplied through the formation of new groups.

Small Groups—Reaching Our World

Small groups can also be an extremely effective tool for reaching the lost. Evangelism ought to be on the priority list of every small group. While it is imperative to pursue progressive sanctification and mutual care, we dare not lose sight of Christ's command to reach our world with the gospel.

Much of today's small-group literature, however, takes an either/or approach—suggesting that small groups can choose to focus on sanctification *or* evangelism, but not both. Yet it is not only possible to do both, God has told us to do both (see Matthew 28:18-20).

I find it fascinating to watch new Christians get involved in the church. They still know more unbelievers than they do Christians, so it's often quite easy for them to reach out effectively to their unsaved friends. They simply invite their non-Christian friends to their new church home and, amazingly, the friends come.

> 66 The test of a congregation, apart from personal holiness, is how effectively members penetrate the world. American churches are filled with pew-sitting, sermon-tasting, spiritual schizophrenics, whose belief and behavior are not congruent.[4] 99
> — **Bill Hull**

Jesus didn't hesitate to befriend sinners, and it worked then, too. When Jesus called Matthew the tax collector to follow him, Matthew invited many of his tax-collector buddies to join him for dinner with Jesus and the disciples (Mt 9:9-13),

86

and Jesus came to be known as the friend of tax collectors and sinners.

I have fond memories of leading small groups that had this sort of opportunity. New believers came in, and suddenly our group was meeting people and ministering in circles to which, previously, we had had no access. We presented the gospel to unsaved (now "ex-") boyfriends and girlfriends, co-workers, friends, and family members. We got to perform bathtub baptisms, help young Christians grow, cry out often for wisdom, and experience the joy of transformed lives in a growing small group. Let this dynamic work for your group...and make way for the newcomers! They are a harvest if you will put in the sickle.

Indeed, there is no reason why a small group cannot maintain a dynamic of mutual care *and* spiritual growth, even while pursuing evangelistic outreach. Here are some ideas that we have implemented in an effort to begin to reach our community. These activities are not evangelism per se—because evangelism is nothing less than the clear and specific presentation of the gospel of Jesus Christ and his finished work on the Cross—but they can lay the groundwork for evangelism by presenting tangible demonstrations of the love of God.

We encourage reaching out to neighbors through service. This means being aware of needs in our neighborhoods and seeking to meet them. Our small groups regularly wash cars for free at a busy local restaurant on Saturdays. It's a great way to serve and get to know people.

Some of the groups have hosted "free garage sales" in their neighborhood. (No junk allowed!) Many church members have testified of significant "death-to-self" experiences as they watch another group member bringing something to be given away which is just what they want or need! Sorry, the customers come first...The "free sales" naturally raise some eyebrows and generate lots of questions. This gives the hosts a chance to explain their motive—to communicate the love of God in a practical way. Conversations like these can lead easily to an invitation to a church meeting, or to a presentation of the gospel.

Two groups had the "bright" idea of a light bulb give-away, and joined forces to make the load "lighter."

Meditate on John 4:35. The "fields" of your community are ripe for harvest!

Meditate on 2 Corinthians 2:14-16; 3:5. God knows exactly whom he will draw to your small group, and he wants your life to attract them to truth.

> 66 People of all kinds come when they have been truly welcomed. But Christ's welcome cannot have a reservation. A smile in the sanctuary is not enough; we must be willing to welcome them into our homes, too.[5] 99
>
> — C. John Miller

When God brings change into my life, my natural response is to resist it. So God puts me in situations where I simply have to adjust.

Last year our pastors decided to multiply our small group. I wanted to stay with my original group. I had been with these same people for six years and had worked through many personal issues with the group's leader. Our group had developed good relationships, new Christians had brought fresh zeal for what God was doing, and the leader was skilled in the Word. I felt I had found my place there.

I talked with church leadership about which group I should be in. They encouraged me that I could add value to either group.

I remembered a challenge from a message I'd heard years earlier: Would I be a pioneer or a settler? As I took that exhortation to heart, God removed my fear of change and replaced it with excitement for the new group I could participate in under new leadership.

I'm glad God did that for me, because this year our small group multiplied and now I'm in yet another one! I've learned that when God adds new groups, it's to bless others and to equip us for carrying out God's mission. I struggled with the idea of change until I realized that God is the God of change. We're resisting him when we don't receive his direction with a grateful and expectant heart.

— Troy Garner (Morton, PA)

Groups have also done free gift-wrapping at Christmas, yard work, and drink giveaways. These are just a few ideas.

We also encourage everyone in our church to reach out to "one life." Many people in our church ask God to show them at least one person to pray for and build a relationship with during the year. The idea is not to set limits on us, but to provide a tangible and easily identifiable goal. It is exciting to watch doors open for the gospel to go forth in families, neighborhoods, and workplaces. It is great to know that small groups as a whole are supporting the individual members as they reach out to "one life." The encouragement, prayer, and accountability available in a small group make a huge difference. As the efforts bear fruit, small groups rally around new Christians with care and encouragement. In these and other ways, God is challenging our church to believe him for greater evangelistic effectiveness.

The Sum of the Parts

Through my involvement as a small-group leader and pastor over the years, I have seen first-hand that the small-group structure has much to do with a church's level of success. This truth does not minimize the importance of doctrine, worship, effective pastoring, or evangelism. But the role of the small group is unique—it represents the practical application of a church's beliefs. Generally, people can only be made an integral part of a church through their small-group involvement; it is rare for this process to be accomplished through Sunday- morning meetings alone.

For a church to be strong and continuing to mature, the members must become wholeheartedly involved in their small group. They must be determined not to plateau or get comfortable with the status quo. Like a mother bird who knows when to push her chicks toward the edge of the nest, God does not want us to stay as we are. He is faithful to challenge us to take that next step of faith.

As individuals, the challenge may be to greater levels of service or evangelism. When a church grows numerically (which is always part of God's intention), small groups may be challenged to release leaders to move into a new phase of ministry; release long-standing members to lead new groups; embrace new members or leaders; or re-form into completely new groups. It is at these times that we find out what we truly believe—whether our vision is for the growth and progress of the church or simply the preservation of our own comfort.

By viewing our small-group involvement in the context of a larger mission and purpose—that of the local church—we keep a proper perspective. Let's determine to pursue the purpose of small groups without hesitation or reluctance of any kind. Doing this involves welcoming and making room for new people, actively caring for one another, creatively reaching out with the gospel, and gladly releasing new leaders and new groups to serve the church effectively. In other words, it means ...

... Never say "comfortable"! ■

GROUP DISCUSSION 1. In this chapter, "koinonitis" is compared to termites eating away homes from the inside out. What does koinonitis "eat away at" inside us?

2. Do you have memories of attending a meeting and feeling like an outsider? What could someone have done to make you feel more welcome?

3. How "visitor-friendly" is your group? Can you think of ways to improve?

4. Does the thought of your group expanding (and eventually multiplying) excite you? Or tempt you to be anxious?

5. Based on the gifts you see in your group, who would you pick as "Most Likely to Lead a New Group?

6. Have you ever been in a "small" group that was too big for its own good? What positive qualities are lost when a group gets too large?

7. Can you describe a particular time in which God wanted to push you "out of the nest" although you felt you weren't ready to fly? Any areas now in which God is encouraging you to take a step of faith?

RECOMMENDED READING

How to Give Away Your Faith by Paul Little (Downers Grove, IL: InterVarsity Press, 1989)

The Soul Winner by Charles Spurgeon (New Kensington, PA: Whitaker House, 1995)

More Than a Carpenter by Josh McDowell (Wheaton, IL: Tyndale House Publishers, 1987)

Spiritual Disciplines for the Christian Life by Donald Whitney (Colorado Springs, CO: NavPress, 1997)

CHAPTER SEVEN

AND NOW FOR THE BIG PICTURE

DAVE HARVEY

T he silence was deafening.

Mark had just been pitched a compelling vision of his future by the next president of a Fortune 500 company. The "vision" involved a lucrative salary, some serious perks, and a position as his personal assistant. Yes sir, opportunity was certainly knocking...more power, more challenge, and plenty of income were only a handshake away.

Many men wait their whole lives for this. At that moment, though, Mark was just searching for a diplomatic way to say, "No thanks."

Don't get me wrong. Mark enjoyed his work and did it with excellence. But he knew that unspoken costs and compromises would accompany this new position. Evenings at the office, weekends away from home, a life preoccupied with business—he mentally reviewed the checklist as his boss waited for his response.

The issue was not just "family values" or time away from his wife. This "opportunity" posed a threat to something which had become part of the fabric of Mark's Christianity and the reason for much of his spiritual growth. In a flash Mark realized this new position might compromise a higher vision God had given him for his life...*a vision to be committed to the local church*.

Mark said no. Four years later, he has no regrets.

Raising Our Sights

What would cause a man to reject such a bright future? The answer is a simple one, but it is also spectacular: Mark was captivated by a biblical vision for the local church—a vision that translated into commitment, even when that commitment meant personal sacrifices. Mark's own words may sum it up best: "God had convinced me there was a higher priority in life. And that's where I wanted to be!"

That higher priority was the local church.

Our reaction to Mark's decision may reveal a lot about our own vision for the local church. Doubtless, some believers would have interpreted the promotion as God's blessing, despite the fact that Mark's church involvement would be seriously compromised by the weekend hours and extra responsibilities. Still others might feel Mark was too "fanatical" in his convictions, that God is most glorified by our moderation toward his church. Some might actually think it more important for Mark to make career growth a higher priority than spiritual growth. (In other words, "Seek first your career and its bounty, and all God's blessings will be added unto you.")

> 44 Perhaps the greatest single weakness of the contemporary Christian church is that millions of supposed members are not really involved at all, and what is worse, do not think it strange that they are not.[1] 77
>
> — **Elton Trueblood**

Not only is such a perspective unbiblical, it is foolishly shortsighted. The most important decision a person will ever make is whether he or she will be devoted to Jesus Christ. And devotion to Jesus cannot be effectively implemented without a devotion to the local church.

Meditate on Matthew 6:33. What are we really supposed to seek first? What are the benefits for those who do?

Throughout this book, you have heard that small groups are not an end in themselves; they are a means for maturing and serving together within a specific local church. For that reason, it seems appropriate that our final chapter look beyond small groups and focus on the church itself. Without a high view of the church, our understanding of small groups will be pitifully incomplete.

Supply and Demand

A few years ago, *Newsweek* ran a cover story on Baby Boomers and religion that dropped a bombshell on the evangelical church. With startling clarity, the piece concluded that "some of the least demanding churches are now in the greatest demand."[2]

That may be true, but it's not healthy, and it's certainly not scriptural. No such statement could ever be made about the church described in Acts. Here we find a "devoted" people willing to forsake the world in order to jump into the community of God's people:

With many other words [Peter] warned them; and

For Further Study:
Jesus minced no words
in describing the cost
of discipleship. Are you
willing to forsake all as
he describes in Luke
9:57-62?

he pleaded with them, "Save yourselves from this
corrupt generation." Those who accepted his message were baptized, and about three thousand were
added to their number that day. They *devoted*
themselves to the apostles' teaching and to the
fellowship, to the breaking of bread and to prayer.
(Ac 2:40-42)

This passage shows a natural three-part progression
which Christians in our day should imitate: 1) come out
of the world, 2) come into the church, and 3) fix your
devotion on divine pursuits. These
three critical steps—*forsaking, addition*, and *devotion*—encompass what it
means to be genuinely committed to
the local church.

> **1** What is one practice you clearly need-
> ed to forsake when you first became
> a Christian?

The "least demanding churches"
may successfully *gather* people who
are ready to forsake the world, but they
won't *build* people into a committed
community. To accomplish that, we
need addition and devotion.

Called Out, Added In

Addition is more than being *mystically* joined to the
universal body of Christ. It also means being *practically*
joined and committed to *one local church*. This is clearly
expressed in the New Testament. How else could Peter
urge pastors to shepherd those "under your care" and
"entrusted to you" (1Pe 5:2-3)? Jesus expresses the same
assumption about the church when explaining how to
deal with someone who sins against you (Mt 18:17).

Historically, commitment to one church has always
been a central feature of the faith—a non-negotiable for
all believers. This commitment has been customarily
expressed through the privilege of church membership.
Throughout the centuries, membership has been the
practical way for pastors to know the boundaries of their
flock so they can protect and care for it.

In the early church, membership was often formalized
through the "sponsor system," in which each prospective
member had to present a witness to act as surety for his
commitment.[4] In fact, membership was so esteemed that
instruction for new members could last up to three years![5]
Captivated by a high view of the church and a biblical
vision for church life, these early believers transmitted to

many generations after them a passion for the local church. But that passion never quite made it to our generation, as D. Martyn Lloyd-Jones observes:

> It is our failure as Christian people to understand what our church membership means—the dignity, the privilege, and the responsibility—that causes most of our troubles. Our greatest need is to recapture the New Testament teaching concerning the Church.[6]

God does not call us out from this "corrupt generation" so we can meander aimlessly over the Christian landscape —a meeting here, a teaching there, some occasional small group involvement just for variety. We have been *called out* to be *added in*! All believers should be committed to a local church that cares for their souls, equips them for ministry, and benefits from their service.

Church can't be a mere accessory. We must be added.

I like Eugene Peterson's translation of the passage we read in Acts: "That day about three thousand took him at his word, were baptized and were signed up" (Ac 2:41). "Signing up" is a great way to describe being added, and being added is absolutely vital—but it's only a start. According to Acts 2, God wants to move each of his children beyond addition to *devotion*.

A Place and Purpose for Devotion

I love it when we have "Commitment Sundays"! These are the services where our church officially receives and honors those whom God is adding to our midst. Before this event, each prospective member has completed a 12-week New Members Course, made a commitment to a small group, and met with a pastor to discuss any questions or concerns. The services are inspiring because we often hear a testimony of how God rekindled a passion for the local church. Recently, Stu and Lisa shared their own odyssey:

> One of the things Lisa and I decided we would do when looking for a church was visit the small-group meetings first, rather than the Sunday-morning service. We knew that was where we would see what the church is really like. So we visited the nearest small group three times, and felt it was the closest thing to New Testament Christianity we had seen in years. So you see, we had already decided to be a part of this church before we ever visited on a Sunday morning!

Stu and Lisa were not looking to play church. They wanted to attach themselves to a "devoted" people—and they knew that devotion which is merely conceptual or theoretical isn't devotion at all, it's daydreaming. (There's no such thing as "virtual" devotion.)

Realistically, devotion requires both a clear goal and a context in which to express itself. The New Testament church was not randomly devoted to every cause, passion, or structure; rather, they were strategically devoted. They expressed that devotion through Temple meetings, home meetings, prayer meetings, and hospitality times, just to name a few. Stu and Lisa discovered a similar dynamic. When they visited their small group, they knew they had found a strategy and a context where they could freely express their devotion to Jesus Christ and his church.

Meditate on Ephesians 2:19-22. Like a master bricklayer, God has built you into the church—and put you there to stay!

How about you? Where is your devotion being expressed? John Stott once said, "Small groups…are indispensable for our growth into spiritual maturity."[7] Have they become indispensable in your life?

Before we leave Stu and Lisa, let me clarify one thing. As much as they love their small group, their primary commitment is to the church. They are devoted to their group *because* it is a strategic extension of church life.

> ❝ While a small group may be part of a church, it is not a substitute for the church.[8] ❞
> — Douglas Wilson

Here's What Devotion Looks Like

So much of the life of a healthy church takes place among its small groups. Where small groups are present, devotion is essential, and can be recognized by the following three ingredients:

For Further Study:
Where do you find churches meeting in Romans 16:5,
1 Corinthians 16:19,
and Colossians 4:15?

Attendance. It's hard to be devoted "in absentia." You'll find your devotion is much more meaningful, and much more recognizable, *if you're actually at the meeting*! Just a small thing—one of those detail items.

Participation. When it comes to small groups, the old adage remains true: "You get out of it what you put into it." Effective participation requires preparation. For example, it requires that you complete assignments and reflect on discussion topics. But more importantly, it means coming prayerfully prepared to apply the subject matter *to your life*. This involves open and honest sharing with the other members. It means taking the initiative to reveal yourself, rather than remaining isolated on the periphery. It means applying the example of Jesus.

As the following verse shows, Jesus revealed himself in a unique way: "No one has ever seen God, but God the One and Only, who is at the Father's side, *has made him known*" (Jn 1:18, emphasis mine). The Greek verb for the italicized phrase is *exegeomai*, meaning "to expound or to reveal."[9] (This is where we get the word "exegesis," a term for interpreting—or revealing—the truth of Scripture.) Do you see John's point here? When it comes to self-revelation, God takes the initiative! He revealed himself by sending his Son into the world. Jesus "exegeted" God—he made him known—by sharing his heart, mission, and life.

**Meditate on Psalm
141:5.** If you had David's attitude, would you find it any easier to reveal yourself to others?

Just as God made himself known through Jesus, so we must make ourselves known to one another. Yet pride tempts us to do the opposite—to cloak our true identity, to hide behind an image. Why? Because it's easy to look good in the dark.

I made that embarrassing discovery one morning at the office. I needed to be at work extra early, so rather than wake my sleeping family, I got dressed in the dark. Congratulating myself for my stealth, I slipped out of the house and drove to my well-lit office—only to find that my shoes didn't match. To make things worse, no one else in the office was surprised! (Long ago they diagnosed me as "fashion-challenged"…some still believe my choice of footwear that day was intentional!)

Anyone can look sharp in the dark. Darkness makes us invisible, obscuring our heart and concealing our actions. But self-revelation illuminates. It exposes who we really are,

2 Are there any "skeletons in your closet"—past sins or current habits—that you would be afraid to share with someone in your small group? Read James 5:16… then ask God how you should respond.

warts and all. Without such honesty and openness, we can never experience true fellowship.

The verse I quoted earlier (John 1:18) has serious implications for small groups. It helps us realize that our success as groups depends on the depth of our self-revelation. To participate fully, we must be willing to open our hearts and become accountable for our actions.

> **Spiritual growth and maturity simply will not happen apart from relationships in the local church...In relationships we develop an accurate assessment of ourselves that is neither too favorable nor too critical. In relationships we experience a God-ordained channel of supply spiritually, intellectually, and emotionally.**[10]
>
> **— C.J. Mahaney**

I'm part of a small group where I get to experience this firsthand on a regular basis. At a recent meeting, we separated the men and women and answered this question: "What known sin have you committed in the past week?" It was a glorious time of fellowship as we honestly "exegeted" ourselves. There's no doubt about it ...the quality of our fellowship depends upon our participation and self-disclosure, even when it's uncomfortable.

Service. Too often, groups spring up to meet a perceived (and often selfish or superficial) set of needs. "Support groups" are especially prone to this. But unless such groups address our *deepest* need—indwelling sin and its consequences—they won't be of much help to anyone.

Small groups are primarily a means of growth. That's not to say needs don't get met, because they regularly do. Small groups are a tremendous source of encouragement. Most often, however, participants find answers for their own problems as they serve one another. We should come to our small groups ready to give, not just to get.

Did you look carefully at the "one another" list in Chapter Two (page 23)? The list is impressive. But it can only be fulfilled as we are relationally connected within the church. Small groups allow us to develop those necessary relationships *and* help position us to obey the "one another's" in practical ways.

For example, in the church I serve, it is customary for small groups to provide new mothers with meals for a week or two after the arrival of a newborn. Financial needs are often met through a matching-funds program based in the small groups. Here, legitimate financial needs are identified and met through the gracious giving of the small-group members. The pastors may then approve an additional distribution from the church bud-

Meditate on Galatians 5:13. How are we to use the freedom we have in Christ?

get. This system replaces undiscerning "welfare style" distributions with a more biblical view of compassion by meeting needs from within a network of established relationships. More importantly, it provides a practical way to "carry each other's burdens" (Gal 6:2).

In addition to serving those in your group, look for opportunities to serve your local community. To encourage you in this, let me share a remarkably unique strategy our church has fine-tuned through a decade of trial and error: Just serve!

Last fall, one of our small groups decided to display God's love to their neighbors with a leaf-raking project. The strategy was straightforward: 1) knock on a neighbor's door, 2) get permission to rake, and 3) rake. Simple, right? Well, one homeowner was so touched by this small act of kindness that she broke down weeping. Though God gets all the glory, this is just a glimpse of the impact a committed group of people can have when gripped with a vision of serving Jesus, his people, and the world. One such group of twelve, known as the disciples—the Dream Team of small groups—permanently altered the course of human history.

Have You Been Infected?

If every church member expressed such devotion within a small group, this book would be irrelevant. But something has happened in the past 1900 years. The church has moved a long way from that stirring picture we see in the Book of Acts. Those first Christians were completely committed. They enjoyed God and one another, while having a dramatic effect on the world around them. They were devoted, they were serving, they were evangelistic.

Yup. Today, things are a bit different.

Never one to shade the truth, Chuck Colson sees the contrast and makes this chilling observation. "While the church may seem to be experiencing a season of growth and prosperity, it is failing to move people to commitment and sacrifice."[11] No greater indictment could be made of us. Commitment and sacrifice were at the heart of the New Testament church. When they are present, God's people flourish. When they are absent, the church becomes distracted, disillusioned, and ultimately defiled.

What makes an entire generation of believers willing to tolerate such a dim reflection of our first-century counterparts? Could it be that our vision has been obscured? Have undetected influences gradually compromised and corrupted our expectations for the church?

To illustrate this point, I need to let you in on a little secret: computers hate me. Maybe they just feel used, because I spend a lot of time with them but have no interest in knowing them personally. But I'm certain they hate me. I know this because they habitually lose critical files or freeze up while I'm trying to get work done. Then they sit there, lifeless, silently mocking me as my indwelling sin turns to "outdwelling" sin.

Our church administrator recently tried to educate me on this issue. His opinion was that my computer didn't hate me (he obviously lacks discernment) and that it probably didn't have a demon (a possibility I have briefly entertained during especially bad incidents). A virus seemed a more likely explanation. He explained how a virus can slip in undetected and conceal itself in the computer. From there it can wreak havoc as it erases memory, confuses programs, or even compromises an entire system.

The analogy of a computer virus may help us understand

> ❝ It is scandalous that so many believers today have such a low view of the church. They see their Christian lives as a solitary exercise—Jesus and me—or they treat the church as a building or a social center. They flit from congregation to congregation—or they don't associate with any church at all. That the church is held in such low esteem reflects not only the depths of our biblical ignorance, but the alarming extent to which we have succumbed to the obsessive individualism of modern culture.[12] ❞
>
> — **Charles Colson**

why today's churches are so often "failing to move people to commitment and sacrifice." Let's look at five common "viruses" which can neutralize our devotion to the church and small groups.

The Church-Lite Virus

Very few Christians have studied what Scripture says about the church. The results have been catastrophic. Instead of being gripped by the biblical picture of the first church and the final Church, we settle for a weak, culturally infected imitation…you know, church-lite: *tastes great, less filling*!

For Further Study: The Book of Ephesians offers an excellent "crash course" on the church. For starters, read Ephesians 1:22, 3:20-21, and 5:25-32.

Where there is little theological conviction, the vision perishes. As biblical conviction grows, however, a sense of necessity grows with it. Are you a parent who finds yourself attending Sunday meetings sporadically? God's Word will help you recapture a passion for the church and transmit it to your children. Are you a single who rarely finds an evening to spend with the small group? Scripture offers a higher vision, one of commitment to biblical fellowship. Why should any of us settle for less when Scripture offers so much more?

The Feelings Virus

Those infected with this virus depend heavily on subjective impressions. For any number of reasons, they just "don't sense" that God wants them to be involved in a certain local church at this time. More often than not, this reveals a sinful desire for independence rather than a higher form of spirituality.

The danger with the "feelings" virus is its subtlety. People may enjoy visiting a church, yet decide against involvement because the church "feels" wrong—too big or too small, too formal or too casual. Inhibited by such subjective impressions, many never find a church that "feels" just right.

Meditate on Hebrews 10:25. Though stated in a gracious way, what is the clear meaning of this passage? Does it matter whether we *feel* like meeting together?

Fortunately, we don't need a subjective "sense" for something that is objectively clear in Scripture. The New Testament repeatedly commands us to be functioning members in a local church. We don't become involved by "feeling" involved, but by obeying God. Once we get our actions in line with God's Word, the feelings often follow.

The Ambition Virus

Chester was the man to call when a computer system crashed, and many companies did just that. At a moment's notice, he could be tapped to fly off somewhere to troubleshoot a technological catastrophe. These trips often netted him big bucks. We're talking BIG BUCKS!! Though his commitment to church life eroded, his bank account and business reputation soared. So he kept winging off to destinations around the country, easing his doubts and uncertainties by pondering the rewards.

Chester had fallen prey to a virus which afflicts many believers. Having established their citizenship in the kingdom, they still define success by worldly standards. Income, education, and advancement take precedence over character, service, and commitment to church life. This often results in the wholesale exchange of the eternal for the temporal—the kingdom for the culture. In such a climate, naked ambition can even appear noble.

> **❝** I'm convinced that if we were to gain God's perspective, even for a moment, and were to look at the way we go through life accumulating and hoarding and displaying things, we would have the same feelings of horror and pity that any sane person has when he views people in a mental asylum endlessly beating their heads against the wall.[13] **❞**
>
> — **Randy Alcorn**

But God graciously pursued Chester. As he explains it, "I went under the blade of the Holy Spirit." He began to see that his craving for riches actually caused him to be a poor investor. Sure, his *money* was invested wisely, but his life and time were being squandered. He was seeking security and significance from wealth rather than obeying God's command to "seek first his kingdom and his righteousness" (Mt 6:33).

Things had to change. And they did.

It started with repentance. Chester identified the sinful root of his ambitious cravings and made thorough confession. Next, he realized his need to be committed to his church and small group. Making changes would not be easy, but he had served his ambitions long enough.

Chester had to believe God in new ways. His convictions were tested as his income shrank and his business underwent a transition. But as so often happens when we're called to walk by faith, the rewards far outweighed the costs.

Chester loves God more than ever. His relationship with his wife has never been stronger or more satisfying.

For Further Study:
Read Matthew 19:27-29. What does Jesus promise to those who sacrifice deeply to follow him?

3 Look carefully at this list. Is there anything here you desire more than pleasing God? (Check any that apply.)

❑ Graduate degree ❑ A higher salary

❑ A fulfilling career ❑ Nobel Prize

❑ A spouse or children ❑ A new home

❑ Approval/respect from others ❑ A company of your own

❑ Godiva chocolate ❑ Other_____

_____

They even found time to have a child, something which didn't seem feasible before the change. Someday, that little girl will rejoice that her father found a passion for the local church.

The Church-Alternative Virus

In my part of the world—maybe in your part, too—we once had a phrase which, like all good phrases, got totally overused. It has since been laid to rest, yet lives on in vocabulary heaven with other worn-out phrases such as "Feelin' groovy" and "Keep on truckin'." The phrase was, "Don't hear what I'm not saying." I resurrect this phrase now to appeal for *careful listening* as we turn our attention to the subject of parachurch ministries.

As I mentioned earlier, few Christians these days have a full and clear understanding of Scripture's teaching on the church. Perhaps the most widespread and perplexing result of our ignorance has been the parachurch phenomenon: the rapid emergence of ministries, agencies, and other organizations which conduct Christian ministry *entirely dislocated from the local church*. Some of these groups actually believe they must remain separate from the church in order to be effective. Not only is this puzzling, but it is profoundly confusing for the Christian who wants to live biblically.

Meditate on Ephesians 3:8-11.
Through what institution is God displaying his manifold wisdom?

Today, new Christians are confronted with a priority crisis. In what context should they express their commitment to God? Who will provide care for their soul and direction for their zeal? Perhaps, they think, Christianity is like a department store. Emotional problems are handled by the Christian Therapy Department. The "missions itch" is scratched in the Evangelism Ministries Section. You can tune into Teaching Ministries in the Electronics Department (TV or radio...you choose!). And fellowship is found in any one of the dozens of specialized Fellowship Groups up on the third floor.

Is this really the New Testament pattern?

Now, please remember that phrase: "Don't hear what I'm not saying!"

The work of a parachurch ministry is legitimate and helpful when it focuses on areas of service that are clearly

> **"** Meta- and Para-organizations often serve useful auxiliary roles, with a scope or specialized purpose different from what a particular local church is able to do. In my view, there are a number of valid roles for cooperative ministries operating in a wider sphere than parish or locale: education, publishing and other mass media, cooperative endeavors to meet particular needs (crisis pregnancy, marriage enrichment, prison, campus, military chaplaincy, etc.), hospitals, international and regional ministries, and carrying a banner for particular causes within the large scope of Christian concerns. *Such extramural Christian works need to remember that they are 'barely legitimate,' in the sense that they ought to exist only when they genuinely and intentionally serve the interests of the communities whose mature functioning will put them out of business.* For example, para-church and meta-church become illegitimate when they compete with or use local churches to their own ends: power, status, wealth, autonomy, etc.[14] **"**
>
> **— David Powlison**

outside the capacity of local churches in a particular geographic area (Wycliffe Bible Translators is a good example). Indeed, Sovereign Grace Ministries benefits from and supports a number of parachurch ministries, and for this we thank God. Even where the activites of parachurch ministries are more "church-like" (and thus less biblical), there is no disputing the well-intentioned efforts of parachurch leaders or the fruit these ministries produce. (As a new believer, my first experience of fellowship was in a parachurch ministry which is still in operation today.) However, it is absolutely essential to realize that *these ministries exist largely because local churches have fallen short of their biblical mandate.* Truly, parachurch ministries are evidence of the unpaid debt of the local church.

Unintentionally, many of these ministries have ignored the New Testament pattern and become an "alternative" to the local church. Where that is the case, a ministry has become a dangerous virus, regardless of intention—or even success. Our respect for these ministries should not keep us from holding them accountable to biblical criteria. Specifically, I see four areas in which parachurch ministries can, in effect, usurp the church's God-given role.

They can create an alternative authority. When personal issues spring up in a believer's life, there is no substitute for the anointed and discerning care of a pastor who has been entrusted with that soul (1Pe 5:2-3). However, in a world of television ministries, Christian counseling centers, and mission agencies, we can easily forget that God has called *pastors* to be our primary source of spiritual oversight.

If a parachurch organization fails to recognize the priority of the local church, it will minimize the importance

For Further Study:
Read Ephesians 4:11-13. Whom has God equipped to lead Christians to unity and maturity?

of pastoral authority and care. One pastor I know was put in an awkward position after counseling a member of his church. Though he had encouraged this individual to accelerate her spiritual growth by getting involved in service opportunities, a Christian counselor ignored the pastor's advice and urged her not to serve. Such collisions are inevitable when the local church is deemphasized and its authority diminished by alternatives.

They can create an alternative structure. The local church is *the* New Testament structure for care, discipleship, and missions. Nothing can replace it. It is a mysterious institution, ordained by God as a means of grace for our growth. Where it is upheld and built, you will see a growing people capable of experiencing New Testament Christianity. Where it is overlooked or marginalized, you tend to find immature, unconnected believers with a shallow understanding of the Gospel.

I find no New Testament examples of ministries that operated independently of local churches. Conference ministries, radio programs, and on-line fellowship can certainly supplement the church, but they are most effective when operating under a church's direction and accountability.

Meditate on Matthew 16:18. What is Jesus determined to build?

In his seminal critique of contemporary evangelicalism, David Wells sees the parachurch explosion as another indication of how "the consumer culture has infiltrated today's evangelical church."[15] He notes that the most profound effect has been on the "*structure* of evangelicalism" and says it "represents a remarkable transformation and decentralization of the evangelical world since the immediate postwar years."[16]

What has the "consumer culture"—as reflected in many parachurch ministries—decentralized us *from*? Nothing less than the primacy of doctrine and the centrality of the local church. Where either of these fall, the other is sure to follow, creating many "good" alternatives which in fact wage war with God's best.

They can create an alternative testimony. The local church is an awesome concept. Confounding the pundits, it can unite people who are diametrically opposed in their passions, preferences, and cultures, creating a brilliant display of unity from diversity. Somehow, our "unified diversity" reflects God's unified diversity, becoming a testimony to our culture of the power of God.

Does parachurch work portray the same testimony? Usually not. The greatest strength of such ministries—their primary focus on specific needs—is likewise their greatest weakness. Specialization keeps them from

For Further Study:
Read 1Corinthians
12:17-20. Does
diversity benefit or
harm your body? How
about Christ's body?

experiencing the marvelous diversity that can characterize the local church.

To Paul, diversity was a strength. Be it gift or function, preference or passion, Paul taught that diversity created interdependence—a *need* for one another's differences (1Co 12:12-26). It would be unimaginable for Paul to encourage any group, whether businessmen or bikers, to establish an identity independent of the local church. Christianity was never meant to be split into "teaching ministries" or "soup kitchens" or "special-interest fellowships." We are the local church, beautifully diverse and powerfully effective.

They can create an alternative storehouse. If you have ever attended a Billy Graham crusade, you have probably heard a statement like this when the offering was collected: "Please don't give any of your tithe to this ministry. That belongs to the local church!" What motivates this commendable and all-too-rare practice? An awareness that the local church—not a parachurch ministry—is God's designated "storehouse" (Mal 3:10).

I don't object to sponsoring a needy child or contributing to hunger relief. However, parachurch programs frequently divert resources (both tithe and time) from the local church. Such appeals lack biblical support. In fact, it is interesting to note that when the Jerusalem church became needy, Paul rallied local churches to give sacrificially. He didn't establish an independent Christian relief agency. Resonating throughout the New Testament is this principle of resources "flowing through" the local church.

> ❝ If the church is central to God's purpose, as seen in both history and the gospel, it must surely also be central to our lives. How can we take lightly what God takes so seriously? How dare we push to the circumference what God has placed at the center?[17] ❞
>
> **— John Stott**

Over the years, parachurch ministries have served many useful purposes. Our church has learned and benefitted from them. But their effectiveness should not keep us from asking some questions. Should we enthusiastically support organizations that have no precedent in Scripture? Is the New Testament pattern, with its emphasis on the church, no longer sufficient? Should we assume that the past effectiveness of parachurch ministries validates their future existence? If we will answer these questions biblically rather than sentimentally or pragmatically, the conclusions we reach may surprise us.

Where capable churches exist or emerge, parachurch ministries should recognize the scriptural legitimacy and primacy of the church. After seeking to equip the local church from their expertise, they should gradually reposition themselves to function under church leadership. To many, this will be a radical suggestion. *But when the simple pattern of Scripture seems radical, we may be certain the church has drifted.*

Meditate on 1 Timothy 3:15. What a powerful description of the church!

What could happen if God married the heroic zeal of parachurch visionaries to a theological conviction for the local church? The church would be revolutionized…and the world might never be the same!

The Leisure Virus

Sasha loves the church—as long as it doesn't interrupt her leisure pursuits. Although she just turned 40, her appetite for fun has grown in proportion to her income and rivals that of a woman half her age. Travel, sports, theater, movies, 500 cable channels…so much to do, so little time. With her high-pressure job, she believes she "needs" these distractions to refresh her weary soul.

Not surprisingly, Sasha's pursuits leave little time for God or his church. At Sunday meetings (when she makes it) she stays on the fringe, often criticizing the service while carefully avoiding anyone who might challenge her lifestyle decisions. Her small-group attendance is erratic. With all her pressures, the last thing she needs is one of those "legalistic" talks about commitment. After all, she became a member, didn't she? And why would God bless her with all these opportunities if he didn't want her to enjoy them?

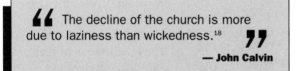

> **"** The decline of the church is more due to laziness than wickedness.[18] **"**
> — John Calvin

Sasha has the "leisure" virus. (The Bible would call it an idol.) It entices Christians to feast at its table and then rewards their gluttony with years of spiritual barrenness. Leisure tempts us to trade our experience of God for the entertainment of men. It makes us mere spectators rather than participants in God's purposes. Leisure subtly persuades us to invest our time, not necessarily in evil, but in *irrelevance.*

For Further Study: If we love the world and its pleasures, how do we feel toward God? (See 1 John 2:15)

Leisure's snare is not so much in its essence as in its indulgence. It's a little like one of those "Magic Fingers" vibrating beds you find in some old motels. It swallows our

106

money and makes us feel good for a short time. But soon that time and money are gone and we're still in the same place.

Where leisure is uncritically enjoyed, the church will transition steadily from prophetic to passive, all the while eloquently justifying its decline. Just ask Sasha.

What Will You Leave Behind?

In his classic message, "Drum Major Instinct," Dr. Martin Luther King, Jr. described his hopes for life and death:

> I won't have any money to leave behind
> I won't have the fine and luxurious things of life to
>   leave behind
> *I just want to leave a committed life behind*
> And that's all I want to say…

As you finish this book, we trust you come away with practical insights and suggestions that will make your small group even better. Our goal in writing it, however, penetrates much deeper. We have tried pointing beyond small groups to the purpose for which they exist—Christ's glorious Bride, the church.

Love your church. Lay down your life for your church. Pour out your passions and energies to accomplish God's plan for the church. Your small group has enormous potential—harness it for the benefit of your church. For this is where God has called you. This is where he is changing you. This is where he wants you to leave a committed life behind.

And that's all I have to say. ■

GROUP DISCUSSION 1. What is one thing you feel so strongly about that you would "pound the table" in a conversation? (Examples: politics, the environment, guinea pig breeding….)

2. Is it really essential that a Christian be part of a church?

3. What expectations does your church have of you?

4. How well does your small group serve each other? … the local church? … the community? Any need for change?

5. Read Ephesians 3:10-11 aloud. What do these verses tell you about the importance of the church?

6. Are you currently pursuing any career goals or hobbies that compromise your commitment and contribution to the church?

7. What is the author's main reason for questioning parachurch ministries?

8. Are you submitted to your pastor's spiritual authority? Would others agree with your assessment?

9. Are you pouring time and energy into anything which, on an eternal scale, is irrelevant?

10. Is the church at the center—or at the circumference—of your affections?

RECOMMENDED READING

The Body by Charles Colson and Ellen Santilli Vaughn (Dallas, TX: Word Publishing, 1992)

The Church by Edmund Clowney (Downers Grove, IL: InterVarsity Press, 1995)

Life in the Father's House by Wayne Mack and David Swavely (Phillipsburg, PA: P&R Publishing, 1996)

Spiritual Disciplines Within the Church by Donald Whitney (Chicago, IL: Moody Press, 1996)

"What It Means to Me"

Walt Russell

The weekly Bible study began with comfortable predictability. After the customary pie, the members got cups of coffee and settled into their familiar niches around the room. Charlie, the leader, cleared his throat to signal that things were starting. As he did with merciless regularity each week, he began with the question, "Well, what do these verses mean to you?"

The discussion followed a familiar pattern. Each responded to what the verses meant to him or her, and the group reached its weekly general consensus—at least on the easier verses. They all knew what was coming, however: another stalemate between Donnell and Maria. Donnell had been a Christian for several years and was the self-appointed resident theologian. For some reason he always seemed to lock horns with Maria, a relatively new Christian, yet an enthusiastic student of the Bible.

The scene repeated itself every time they came to difficult verses. The passage would elicit conflicting interpretations. Donnell would argue vehemently for the interpretation of his former pastor, which usually seemed a bit forced to the rest of the group. But it was Maria, being new and perhaps more straightforward, who would challenge Donnell. Because she didn't know the Bible that well yet, she would relate the difficult verse to her Christian experience in a way that contradicted Donnell's interpretation. Donnell would only redouble his efforts.

The stalemate usually ended with Charlie, the leader, or Betty, the resident peacemaker, bringing "resolution" to the discussion. One of them would calmly conclude by saying, "Well, this is another example of how reading the Bible is a matter of personal interpretation and how a verse can mean one thing to one person and something else to another." The group members would leave with a vague, hollow feeling in their chests.

A recent Barna Research Group survey on what Americans believe confirms what this brief scenario illustrates: we are in danger of becoming a nation of relativists. The Barna survey asked, "Is there absolute truth?" Amazingly, 66 percent of American adults responded that they believe that "there is no such thing as absolute truth; different people can define truth in conflicting ways and still be correct." The figure rises to 72 percent when it comes to those between the ages of 18 and 25.

Before we stoop to cast the first stones, we evangelicals might ask if we are without sin in this matter, especially when it comes to our approach to interpreting the Bible. I believe we may unwittingly contribute to the widespread malaise of relativistic thinking. Indeed, our big educational standbys—Sunday school, the adult Bible study, and the sermon—may help spread the disease.

A Mouthful of Confusing Signals

"What does this verse mean to you?" It is stunning how often we use this cliché to signal the beginning of the interpretive time in Bible studies and Sunday-school classes. But the question may send a mouthful of confusing signals.

First, it confuses the "meaning" of a passage with the "significance" of the passage. This point has been cogently made by literary critic E.D. Hirsch, Jr., in his book *Validity in Interpretation*. Hirsch asserts that "*meaning* is that which is represented by a text; it is what the author meant... *Significance*, on the other hand, names a relationship between that meaning and a person, or a conception, or a situation, or indeed anything imaginable."

The meaning of a text never changes. Our first goal is to discover this fixed thing. In contrast, the *significance* of that text to me and to others is very fluid and flexible.

> **❝** The meaning of a text never changes. Our first goal is to discover this fixed thing. In contrast, the *significance* of that text to me and to others is very fluid and flexible. **❞**

By confusing these two aspects of the interpretation process, we evangelicals approach the Bible with an interpretive relativism. If it means one thing to you and something contradictory to me, we have no ultimate court of appeals. We can never establish and validate "the one correct interpretation." In fact, our language and approach suggest that there is no such animal.

In conservative Christian circles this has tragically led to people seeing the authority of God residing in the most powerful preachers of his Word rather than in the Word itself. This explains Donnell's appeal, "But *my pastor* says...."

Second, the question "What does this verse mean to you?" reflects a drift in determining meaning that has been going on for a century in literary circles. The classical approach was to focus on *the author* and his or her historical and (later) emotional setting in life. Earlier in the twentieth century the focus shifted to *the text*, and authors lost their special rights to explain what their text meant. Texts allegedly take on a life of their own apart from their authors.

However, the drift has not stopped at the text. The focus for determining meaning is now on *the interpreter*. The reader allegedly "creates meaning."

Applied to biblical study, interpretation becomes not discovering the absolute truths of God's Word, but winning others over to what the text "means to us" because our system for explaining it is the most internally coherent and satisfying. The best we can hope for us to persuade others to join our interpretive community, at least until a more coherent and satisfying interpretation comes along.

Within academic circles, this emphasis on creating meaning has been broadly labeled "reader-response criticism." It has had an enormous impact on many disciplines within both the university community and our broader culture, from the interpretation of literature to the interpretation of the U.S. Constitution.

Avoiding Relativism

What can we do to avoid this relativism?

First, we need to clean up our language when we talk about Scripture. If we want to discuss the *meaning* of the text, then we ask, "What does this verse or text mean?" If we want to discuss *significance*, then ask, "What is the relevance or significance of this verse to you?"

Second, we must differentiate between our *emotional posture* (tolerant and sensitive) and *our view of the truth* (something absolute, which can be determined). We show sensitivity but avoid giving up too much "real estate."

> ❝ We must differentiate between our *emotional posture* (tolerant and sensitive) and *our view of the truth* (something absolute, which can be determined)....When disagreements arise, it is tempting to retreat from the hard work under the banner of tolerance and sensitivity. Instead, we should underscore in a loving, sensitive manner that only one of several conflicting interpretations can be correct. ❞

Establishing correct meanings entails lots of hard, interpretive work. When disagreements arise, it is tempting to retreat from the hard work under the banner of tolerance and sensitivity. Instead, we should underscore in a loving, sensitive manner that only one of several conflicting interpretations can be correct. This correct interpretation can be validated as the most likely one primarily by arguing from the main theme of the passage's immediate context.

We who teach the Bible feel the pressure Americans generate for immediate application. We are therefore constantly tempted to skip the hard work of determining a biblical text's meaning and move quickly to the text's personal relevance. We should ask, "When was the last time we took the time during teaching a passage to establish its context?" Such work will take up part of our teaching time, and it is difficult to make the historical or literary contexts "sizzle." The challenge is to make the setting of other people's lives and questions as interesting as our own.

Many of us are unwilling to establish the passage's literary context by tracing the biblical book's argument. Or we do not establish the historical context by reading background material in a Bible dictionary, a Bible encyclopedia, or a good commentary.

Why? Increasingly we do not see value in establishing a passage's historical and literary context. In believing that God's Word directly addresses us, we ignore that he speaks to our needs *through* the historical and literary contexts of the people of the Bible.

But the reward for such work is that we have the controls and safeguard of the original context that the Holy Spirit used when he inspired the passage. The absence of such work increases our chances of emerging with wrong meaning, wrong emphasis, and wrong application. It may even negate the Holy Spirit's power in our teaching of that passage.

Focusing on the felt needs of listeners makes it easy to end up with a great felt need desperately in search of a passage. The current emphasis on shorter topical preaching and topical Bible studies may unwittingly help feed this relativism in application. The mistake is a fundamental one: elevating the hearers' context over the Bible's. Instead of holding the Bible's context and our contemporary context in a dynamic tension, we assume that the contemporary context is the most important one.

This perspective may be more dangerous than we think. It presupposes an existential and human-centered world view. Therefore, the onus is upon each individual to wring some sense of life through the exercise of personal choice. If we unwittingly cater to this world view, God and his Word become reduced to helpful items on life's smorgasbord of options that bring fulfillment.

It would be far better to appeal to a genuine felt need and then challenge the world view that surrounds that need. Our culture's context—an existential, human-centered world view—needs to be confronted by the Bible's context—a historical and God-centered world view. Verses isolated from their literary contexts seldom achieve such a confrontation. Whole paragraphs discussed within the flow of broader arguments come much closer.

> **❝** Focusing on the felt needs of listeners makes it easy to end up with a great felt need desperately in search of a passage....The mistake is a fundamental one: elevating the hearers' context over the Bible's. Instead of holding the Bible's context and our contemporary context in a dynamic tension, we assume that the contemporary context is the most important one. **❞**

Sprinkling single verses into the topical sermon or tacking them on at the end of a "need-oriented" Bible study do not point the listener to the God of the text, but to the teacher of the text. This is especially likely to happen with baby-boomer listeners, who tend to be more person oriented than authority oriented.

Our Needs are Not Enough

An example of how this works can best be illustrated by an approach to a four-part Bible-study series in light of Americans' strong felt need for happiness.

We might remember that Paul's letter to the Philippians was about "joy" and "rejoicing." A quick read confirms the presence of those words. We have already determined our general *targeted need* in this series (people's hunger for happiness), and we have already assumed our general *conclusion* for the series (God wants to meet our need for happiness). Therefore, what we are really looking for are interesting and specific biblical bridges from our targeted need to our conclusion. So far, so good. But here is where the weeds get taller and the briars sharper.

We first face a choice about how much time and energy we are going to spend on uncovering the historical, cultural, and literary backgrounds of the Epistle to the Philippians. It seems straightforward enough: True happiness and joy come from knowing Christ and thereby being able to rejoice in any circumstances. A four-part Bible-study series might look like this:

- Joy in friendships *(Phil 1:3-5)*
- Joy in perseverance *(Phil 1:25-26)*
- Joy in teamwork *(Phil 2:1-4)*
- Joy in God's peace (with a low-key evangelistic twist) *(Phil 4:4-7)*

Here we have an expository series with some continuity from one book of the Bible (this satisfies the older folks in the group). We address significant emotional felt needs of both non-Christians and Christians within our culture (this satisfies the baby boomers). And we address some of the key issues people face (this satisfies the baby busters).

But instead of doing the hard work of investigating the epistle's historical and literary context, we made the mistake of assuming *our context* was the main context that mattered. We thereby distorted the meaning of these four passages.

The existential perspective, for example, sets up happiness or joy as the goal. We also distort Paul's understanding of the gospel in Philippians if we interpret this epistle from our fulfillment-fixation perspective. If personal joy and peace are our primary concerns, the gospel is reduced to the God-given means for achieving this kind of fulfillment. It becomes an existential fix-all.

But the biblical perspective sees joy as a by-product of involvement in the gospel cause. By interpreting Paul's eight uses of the word *gospel* in Philippians within their original literary and historical context, we see that the gospel was something in which the Philippians shared in partnership (1:5) and in which Euodia and Syntyche shared Paul's struggle (4:2-3). The gospel was something Paul defended and confirmed (1:7), and which supplied the standard for the Philippians' conduct as they strove for the faith of it (1:27). Ironically, Paul's present sufferings turned out for the greater progress of the gospel (1:12), and Timothy's serving of Paul helped further the gospel (2:22).

The gospel, then, is not something that exists solely for *our progress* and personal fulfillment (although it does include these things). Rather, the gospel is something to which we are to give ourselves for *its* progress and fulfillment. The gospel is God's program for worldwide blessing.

> ❝ The gospel, then, is not something that exists solely for *our progress* and personal fulfillment (although it does include these things). Rather, the gospel is something to which we are to give ourselves for *its* progress and fulfillment. ❞

Only entering into the cultural, historical, and literary context of Philippians allows us to grasp this insight. It requires bridging significant temporal, cultural, and language gaps. But isn't this why God has given the church Spirit-gifted teachers who can take advantage of the embarrassment of riches in Bible-study tools and helps?

A brief visit to a good Christian bookstore will quickly reinforce the fact that no other people in the history of the church have been blessed with our dizzying array of Bible-study aids. Our nemesis is not a lack of resources but a lack of understanding about their necessity.

We must establish the original historical and literary context of biblical passages. Once this work is done, *then* we can move to determining the needs a passage addresses. But *the text*, not our concerns, initially determines the focus. To ignore the necessity of this task is to risk sliding into relativism. We find few contextual safeguards in this land of "what-it-means-to-me" and probably very little of God's voice.

Walt Russell is associate professor of New Testament language and literature at Talbot School of Theology, Biola University, La Mirada, California. This article first appeared in the October 26, 1992 issue of Christianity Today. *Used by permission of the author.*

NOTES ### CHAPTER ONE – Why Small Groups?

1. Sir Arthur Conan Doyle, "A Scandal in Bohemia" in *The Complete Sherlock Holmes* (New York: Doubleday, 1927).
2. J.I. Packer, *God's Words* (Downers Grove, IL: InterVarsity Press, 1981), p. 193.
3. Wayne Grudem, *Systematic Theology* (Grand Rapids, MI: Zondervan Publishing House, 1994), p. 746.
4. Ibid., p. 723.
5. Sinclair Ferguson, *The Christian Life: A Doctrinal Introduction* (Carlisle, PA: The Banner of Truth Trust, 1989), pp. 82-83.
6. Bruce Milne, *Know the Truth* (Downers Grove, IL: InterVarsity Press,1982), p. 194.
7. R.C. Sproul, *The Soul's Quest for God* (Wheaton, IL: Tyndale House Publishers, 1992), p. 151.
8. Quoted by Ralph W. Neighbour, Jr., in *Where Do We Go from Here? A Guidebook for Cell Group Churches* (Houston, TX: Touch Publications, 1990), pp. 166-67.
9. *Newsweek*, March 26, 1990.
10. Peter H. Davids, *New International Bible Commentary: James* (Peabody, MA: Hendrickson Publishers, 1989), p. 41.
11. Gordon Fee, *God's Empowering Presence* (Peabody, MA: Hendrickson Publishers, Inc., 1994), p. 8.
12. Richard F. Lovelace, *Dynamics of Spiritual Life* (Downers Grove, IL: InterVarsity Press, 1979), p. 131.
13. Jerry Bridges, *The Discipline of Grace* (Colorado Springs, CO: NavPress, 1994), p. 35.
14. Wayne Grudem, *Systematic Theology*, p. 635.
15. J. Rodman Williams, *Renewal Theology: Salvation, the Holy Spirit, and Christian Living* (Grand Rapids, MI: Zondervan Publishing House, 1990), p. 305.

CHAPTER TWO – Fellowship Rediscovered

1. J.I. Packer, *God's Words* (Downers Grove, IL: InterVarsity Press, 1981).
2. Jerry Bridges, *True Fellowship* (Colorado Springs: NavPress, 1985), p. 16-17.
3. J.I. Packer, *God's Words*, p. 198-199.
4. George Swinnock, *The Golden Treasury of Puritan Quotations* (Carlisle, PA: The Banner of Truth Trust, 1989) p. 245.

CHAPTER THREE – Take This Group and Own It!

1. Brent Detwiler, "Entering the Promised Land Together," *People of Destiny*, September/October 1995, p. 11.
2. Ibid.
3. Richard Foster, *Celebration of Discipline* (San Francisco, CA: Harper & Row, 1988), p. 153.
4. Dietrich Bonhoeffer, *Life Together* (San Francisco, CA: Harper & Row, 1954), p. 116.
5. Jack Deere, *Surprised by the Power of the Spirit* (Grand Rapids, MI: Zondervan Publishing House, 1993), p. 166.

CHAPTER FOUR – What Makes a Great Leader?

1. Bruce Milne, *Know the Truth* (Downers Grove, IL: InterVarsity Press, 1982), p. 249.

2. Fred Smith, *Learning to Lead* (Wheaton, IL: Christianity Today, Inc., 1986), p. 15.
3. Richard Baxter, *The Reformed Pastor* (Portland, OR: Multnomah Press, 1982), p. 22.
4. Wayne Grudem, *Systematic Theology* (Grand Rapids, MI: Zondervan Publishing House, 1994), pp. 467-68.
5. Jerry Bridges, *The Discipline of Grace* (Colorado Springs, CO: NavPress, 1994), p. 18.

CHAPTER FIVE – The Art of Care and Correction
1. Wayne Grudem, *Systematic Theology* (Grand Rapids, MI: Zondervan Publishing House, 1994), p. 756.
2. Jay Adams, *Solving Marriage Problems*, (Grand Rapids, MI: Zondervan Publishing House, 1983), p. 99.
3. Ken Sande, *The Peacemaker* (Grand Rapids, MI: Baker Book House, 1991), p. 20.
4. Wayne Mack, *Your Family, God's Way* (Phillipsburg, NJ: Presbyterian and Reformed Publishing Co., 1991), p. 170.
5. Terry Virgo, *Restoration in the Church* (Columbia, MO: Cityhill Publishing, 1989), p. 72.
6. E. Bradley Beevers, "Watch Your Language," *The Journal of Biblical Counseling*, Vol. XII, No. 3, Spring 1994, p. 25.
7. Ken Sande, *The Peacemaker*, p. 97.
8. Ibid., p. 164.

CHAPTER SIX – Never Say Comfortable!
1. Charles Bridges, *The Christian Ministry* (Carlisle, PA: The Banner of Truth Trust, 1991), pp. 129-130.
2. Jerry Bridges, *The Crisis of Caring* (Phillipsburg, NJ: Presbyterian and Reformed Publishing Co., 1985), p. 173.
3. John R.W. Stott, *The Message of Ephesians* (Downers Grove, IL: InterVarsity Press, 1979), p. 167.
4. Bill Hull, *The Disciple-Making Pastor* (Old Tappan, NJ: Fleming H. Revell, 1988), p. 20.
5. C. John Miller, *Powerful Evangelism for the Powerless* (Phillipsburg, NJ: P&R Publishing, 1997)

CHAPTER SEVEN – And Now for the Big Picture
1. Quoted by Bill Hull in *The Disciple-Making Pastor* (Old Tappan, NJ: Fleming H. Revell, 1988), p. 19.
2. Quoted by Charles Colson and Ellen Santilli Vaughn in *The Body* (Dallas, TX: Word Publishing, 1992), p. 42.
3. David Wells, *God in the Wasteland* (Grand Rapids, MI: Wm. B. Eerdmans Publishing Co., 1994), p. 226.
4. Lyman Coleman, *Ancient Christianity Exemplified* (Philadelphia, PA: Lippincott, Grabo & Co., 1853), pp. 404-405.
5. Kenneth Scott Latourette, *A History of Christianity*, Vol. 1 (San Francisco, CA: Harper & Row, 1975), p. 195.
6. D. Martyn Lloyd-Jones, *Christian Unity: An Exposition of Ephesians 4:1 to 16* (Grand Rapids, MI: Baker Book House, 1981), p. 209.
7. Quoted by Terry Virgo in *Restoration in the Church* (Eastbourne: Kingsway Publications, 1985), p. 75.
8. David Hagopian and Douglas Wilson, *Beyond Promises: A Biblical Challenge to Promise Keepers* (Moscow, ID: Canon Press, 1996), p. 221.

9. Gerhard Kittel, *Theological Dictionary of the New Testament* (Grand Rapids, MI: Eerdmans, 1985), p. 303.

10. C.J. Mahaney, "It Takes Two," *People of Destiny*, July/August 1991, pp. 2-3.

11. Charles Colson and Ellen Santilli Vaughn, *The Body*, p. 31.

12. Ibid., p. 276.

13. Randy Alcorn, "Materialism: A Great American Snare," *People of Destiny*, March/April 1991, p. 16.

14. David Powlison, "Counseling in the Church" *The Journal of Biblical Counseling* Winter 2002, Vol. 20, No. 2, p. 3, footnote 2. (emphasis added)

15. David Wells, *God in the Wasteland*, p. 62.

16. Ibid.

17. John R.W. Stott, *The Message of Ephesians* (Downers Grove, IL: InterVarsity Press, 1979), pp. 26-27.

18. John Calvin, *The Crossway Classic Commentaries: Acts* (Wheaton, IL: Crossway Books, 1995), p. 50.

DISCIPLINES FOR LIFE
C.J. Mahaney and John Loftness

Are you satisfied with the depth of your devotional life? If you're like most Christians, probably not. *Disciplines for Life* puts change within your grasp. Leave the treadmill of spiritual drudgery behind as you discover fresh motivation and renewed passion to practice the spiritual disciplines. (Paperback, 96 pages)

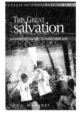

THIS GREAT SALVATION
C.J. Mahaney and Robin Boisvert

Countless Christians struggle through life feeling condemned and confused. No matter how much they do for God, they never feel quite sure of his acceptance. Sound at all familiar? Then you'll find great news in *This Great Salvation*. Start enjoying a new measure of grace and peace at every level of your Christian life as this unique book reveals all God has done for you through Christ. (Paperback, 112 pages)

HOW CAN I CHANGE?
C.J. Mahaney and Robin Boisvert

How Can I Change? rests on a remarkable promise: If you will study and apply the doctrine of sanctification, any sin can be overcome. Have you known the frustration of falling short in your efforts to please God? Have you questioned whether you will ever be able to change? If so, this book can have a profound impact on your walk with Christ. (Paperback, 112 pages)

THE RICH SINGLE LIFE
Andrew Farmer, foreword by Joshua Harris

How do you live your life as a Christian single? Are you aiming at something better than just continually coping? God intends the season of your singleness to be one of great richness, focus, and fulfillment in him—a time when abundance joins hands with opportunity, and your identity in Christ emerges from undivided devotion to the Lord. While acknowledging the unique challenges the single life can pose, this book applies the truth and the heart of Scripture in a way that is inspiring, encouraging, and practical. (Paperback, 176 pages)

OTHER BOOKS FROM SOVEREIGN GRACE MINISTRIES

www.SovereignGraceStore.com

Living the Cross Centered Life
Keeping the Gospel the Main Thing
C.J. Mahaney
Sometimes the most important truth is the easiest to forget.
(Hardcover, 176 pages)

Worship Matters
Leading Others to Encounter the Greatness of God
Bob Kauflin
What a worship leader does, and how to do it well.
(Paperback, 304 pages)

Love That Lasts
When Marriage Meets Grace
Gary & Betsy Ricucci
A biblical, gospel-centered approach to marriage.
(Paperback, 160 pages)

Humility
True Greatness
C.J. Mahaney
Humility and pride cannot coexist—which will you pursue?
(Hardcover, 176 pages)

Feminine Appeal
Seven Virtues of a Godly Wife and Mother
Carolyn Mahaney
Teaching women the specifics of practical living that glorifies God.
(Paperback, 188 pages)

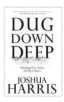

Dug Down Deep
Unearthing What I Believe and Why It Matters
Joshua Harris
Orthodoxy isn't just for scholars—it's for anyone who longs to know the living Jesus Christ.
(Hardcover, 256 pages)

WORSHIP MUSIC FROM SOVEREIGN GRACE MINISTRIES

www.SovereignGraceMusic.org

Sovereign Grace Ministries produces music designed to help churches sing the praise of our great and merciful God. Most of our music is available as MP3 or PDF downloads. Here are just a few of our music resources.

Sons & Daughters
Songs to draw your heart to the unfathomable love God has shown in adopting us through Jesus Christ.

Psalms
New songs echoing the psalmists' passion, prayer, and praise.

Walking with the Wise
Twelve songs for kids based on the book of Proverbs.

Come Weary Saints
Songs to renew your soul and encourage your trust in the sovereign God.

Valley of Vision
Songs inspired by the classic book of Puritan prayers. (www.ValleyofVision.org)

The Worship Songbook Set
Twenty-four years of songwriting. 329 songs. Nearly every song Sovereign Grace has published from 1984 to the *Psalms* album (published in 2008), including Mark Altrogge's "I Stand in Awe" and Vikki Cook's "Before the Throne of God Above."

"Singing and knowing. Rejoicing and reasoning. Delight and doctrine. That's Sovereign Grace Ministries! It is so rare, and so needed....So sing on, Sovereign Grace! And whatever you do, don't stop studying and thinking and preaching about our great Savior." —John Piper, pastor and author

SELECTED AUDIO MESSAGES

www.SovereignGraceStore.com

Sovereign Grace Ministries produces audio series on a number of topics, ideal for personal and small-group application. Many are available in audio CD format, and all are available as free MP3 downloads. Here are just a few.

Pastors Conference 2010
Kevin DeYoung, Dave Harvey, C.J. Mahaney, and others teach on leadership in the local church, with specific application for pastors and their wives.

Next 2010
Seven sessions on essential doctrines of the Christian faith, from Sovereign Grace Ministries' conference for singles and young married couples. With teaching from D.A. Carson, Kevin DeYoung, Mark Dever, Jeff Purswell, C.J. Mahaney, and Joshua Harris.

Together for the Gospel 2010
Mark Dever, Ligon Duncan, C.J. Mahaney, Albert Mohler, Thabiti Anyabwile, Matt Chandler, John MacArthur, John Piper, and R.C. Sproul study and celebrate the glorious gospel and its centrality to the task of pastoring.

WorshipGod09
Thirty messages from Sovereign Grace Ministries' 2009 worship conference. With teaching from John Piper, Bob Kauflin, C.J. Mahaney, and others.

Visit our online store for a complete listing of all our resources.

www.SovereignGraceStore.com

Sovereign Grace Ministries
7505 Muncaster Mill Road
Gaithersburg, MD 20877
resources@sovgracemin.org
800.736.2202